SCREEN TIME
STANDOFF

What experts are saying:

"Screen Time Standoff is a helpful and easy-to-understand guide for families dealing with digital device use. It gives practical advice for creating healthy screen habits, balancing device time, and building real-life connections. With simple tips and real-life examples, the book helps parents and kids find a healthy balance with technology. Clayton does a wonderful job sharing his knowledge in this book, making it a great guide for all parents. Highly recommended!"

— *Edit Alaverdyan, MS. AMFT.*

"Screen Time Standoff is a must read for all parents. Phone and screen use is the biggest conflict in my mental health work with youth and their families. Clayton explores the risks of social media, how to support your child in making healthy choices, and ways to get ahead of conflict with your teen. In this book, adults can learn how to improve their communication with the young people in their lives and learn new techniques to diffuse escalating conflict about screen time. This easy to read and understand guide provides easy to implement techniques that can improve your relationships with your children."

— *Susan Parmelee, LCSW, Director of Wellness & Prevention Center*

"As a school resource officer and parent, Clayton Cranford has witnessed the profound impact smartphones and social media have had on young lives. Screen Time Standoff moves beyond the familiar warnings about the youth mental health crisis, offering parents and educators actionable, results-driven strategies for change. Combining powerful personal narratives with meticulous research, Cranford provides a clear path forward, grounded in solutions rather than fear. Drawing from his frontline experience and data-driven insights, this book is not just timely—it's essential for protecting children's mental health in a digital world."

— *Aniko Hill, Executive Director of kids' digital wellness nonprofit DopaMind*

NEGOTIATION SKILLS
TO UNPLUG YOUR KID

SCREEN TIME STANDOFF

CLAYTON CRANFORD

Dedication

To my wife and best friend, Gretchen, and my two boys,
Clay and Zachary.

Your love, support, and presence in my life have shaped
me into the man I am today. I am forever grateful for the
joy, strength, and inspiration you bring into my world
every single day. I couldn't have done any of this without
all of you.

Books also by Clayton Cranford

Parenting in the Digital World, 3rd Ed.

Educando a Los Padres en el Mundo Digital

Contents

Preface

Thank you for embarking on a transformative journey with Screen Time Standoff. With over two decades of experience in law enforcement, including my time as a Sergeant with the Orange County Sheriff's Department in California, my focus has always been safeguarding our youth. My roles ranged from school resource officer and juvenile investigator on the school threat assessment team to a member of the crisis negotiation team. But above all, I'm a father of two boys who grew up with smartphones, social media, and online gaming. I understand the challenges you face as a parent in this digital age.

As a father, I've walked the path many of you are on. I raised two boys during the early 2010s—when the world of technology was exploding and smartphones were becoming a staple in every teenager's life. Back then, my boys were in elementary and middle school, right at the heart of this digital revolution. The release of the iPhone 4 in 2010, with its forward-facing camera, marked a turning point. By 2015, smartphones were in the hands of over 80% of teens, and this was just the beginning of what Jonathan

Haidt termed the "rewiring of our children's brains" in his book The Anxious Generation.

This shift from face-to-face relationships to online connections was significant. Gaming, which had long been a source of fun and friendship for teens, particularly boys, evolved dramatically. In the early 2000s, games became more social, with multiplayer online games emerging as one of the primary ways young people interacted with their peers. For my boys and countless others, these digital spaces were where they connected, competed, and communicated.

My second perspective on this issue comes from my time as a school resource officer in a city with 14,000 students during the early 2010s. The most frequent causes of disciplinary issues and extreme behavior problems in schools stemmed from online games and social media. Day after day, I dealt with situations where a good kid made a bad choice, often because their parents were unaware of what was happening in their child's digital world.

This experience was the driving force behind the creation of Cyber Safety Cop. Since 2012, we've been visiting schools, speaking to students in assemblies, and holding seminars for parents about the internet, social media, and the effects of gaming. I wrote my first book, Parenting in the Digital World, in 2014, and it has since gone through two more editions and been translated into Spanish. Parenting in the Digital World provides families a step-by-step guide to making their children safer online. After more than a decade of doing this work and speaking to hundreds of thousands of students and tens of thousands of parents, one truth has become abundantly clear: the most important tool a parent can have to help their child be safer and healthier online is the ability to communicate effectively.

This brings me to my third perspective—my experience as a crisis negotiator. It turns out that the skills used in crisis negotiations are exactly what parents need to navigate their children's online habits. As a negotiator, they called me in when someone barricaded themselves inside a building surrounded by the police. The first thing you learn is forcefully ordering someone to come out doesn't work. They have options—they don't have to come out. The key to getting them to comply is to connect with them, make them feel heard, and offer them options that give them a sense of control over their choices.

The same principles apply to parenting in the digital world. Your teen doesn't respond well to orders or ultimatums because, like the person in a standoff, they have options. They are digital ninjas. They can circumvent your parental controls or access the internet and gaming from various sources outside your control. They need to know that we understand them, value their voice, and provide them with choices that empower them to make their own decisions. Ultimately, you want to recruit them as an ally in your endeavor to make them healthier and more responsible.

After talking to thousands of parents, we've uncovered the fundamental challenge all parents struggle with: getting their child to limit their screen time. After my parent seminars I have parents lining up to ask me, "How do I convince my child that being online all day isn't good for them?" or "How can I reduce the battles and frustration when I ask my child to put the game controller down?"

I have a solution that will truly work for you. I will teach you the proven techniques used by hostage and crisis negotiators to defuse even the most chaotic situations: getting a person in crisis to listen and ultimately agree to comply. The communication patterns we instinctively rely on won't help; they often make things worse. We need to adopt a new way of communicating.

This course will explain the role of smartphones and social media in the declining mental health of our children. I'll break down how social media and gaming are hijacking your child's brain and why it can lead to addiction. I will equip you with several powerful communication tools I used as a crisis negotiator, complete with real-life examples that can reduce defensiveness, increase compliance, and overcome objections. Plus, I'll guide you through a step-by-step blueprint for setting effective screen time boundaries, whether your child is young or a teenager. We'll also discuss how to know if your child's online cravings have reached the point of addiction and when it might be time to seek professional help for your child.

If you purchased this book on its own from our website, we offer a companion video series called "Screen Time Standoff" to enhance your learning experience. Use the discount code: "screentimehalfoff", to get the video series at 50% off the regular price.

Let's get started!

Chapter One

My Introduction to Digital Device Addiction

In 2012, two years after the release of the iPhone 4 with a front camera, I served as a school resource officer in Rancho Santa Margarita, California. I had nine schools and fourteen thousand students in my city. I observed the infiltration of smartphones into the lives of teens and preteens as it occurred. I noticed a significant increase in the time teenagers spent glued to their phones and the associated problems. My intermediate school, of more than a thousand students, changed their phone policy from no use during school hours to allowing students to use them during their lunch break. When I stepped into the lunch area, I was taken aback and couldn't believe what I saw. The school's lunch period changed from a raucous forty-five minutes of students chatting and scurrying around the student common area to a kind of zombie land. Students craned their heads down at their screens with little interpersonal interaction. The smiles, eye contact, and laughter were gone. The silence was unsettling.

I was constantly dealing with instances of cyberbullying, issues with online predators, and excessive screen time, leading to academic and social issues among my students. As a result, I acted—and I came up with a plan to educate parents and students on managing screen time and using technology responsibly. This issue was personal to me. I was a parent of two boys who wanted to be online and connected to their peers like every other child their age. I realized the need and the struggle to balance screen time and other activities in my home. This was the beginning of Cyber Safety Cop. Twelve years later, we speak to students and parents throughout the United States. You'd think after twelve years, students would make better choices online and parents would be more engaged in their children's digital world. In every metric of teen online safety and mental health, things have gotten worse.

During a February morning, I stood outside my intermediate school alongside John Bajorek, the school's assistant principal. We were discussing the latest cyberbullying incident that had occurred the day before, while watching parents drop off their kids. This was a great way to connect with my school administrator, brainstorm about issues we were dealing with, and greet the students and parents as they arrived. John's radio crackled to life. I could hear the voice of the front desk receptionist requesting me to come to the front office. A parent called and requested to talk to me. I quickly excused myself and headed to the front office. As I picked up the phone, I could hear the worry and frustration in the parent's voice as she explained her child, Joel, was refusing to go to school. I was familiar with Joel. He was a special needs student and had been in John's office several times for behavior issues. I had sat in on several conversations and knew Joel struggled with impulsiveness and social skills and isolated himself. Sarah, Joel's mother, asked if I would come to their apartment and talk to Joel.

When I arrived at Joel and Sarah's apartment, Sarah welcomed me at the entrance. I could see the sadness, frustration, and weariness in her eyes. As we sat in the living room, Sarah explained Joel had been spending countless hours on his tablet and desktop computer. He was isolating himself in his room all day, playing games on his devices. When Joel was an infant, he suffered a brain injury that led to a diagnosis of severe ADHD and significant learning challenges. Sarah told me she had tried setting limits on Joel's screen time, but he would become highly agitated and defiant when she tried to remove his devices. She said when she tried to take his tablet away the previous night; he jumped onto her back and pried the tablet out of her hands. This was new. He had never physically confronted her before, and now she was scared. According to her, he expressed a desire to stay home and play games. She tried to encourage him to go to school, but a flash of anger met her, reminding her of the previous night. She had to work and couldn't leave him home alone. Sarah worked two jobs to afford to live in Rancho Santa Margarita, so that her son could attend a good school and live in a safe city. I asked her if she wanted me to help her. She nodded as tears welled up in her eyes.

Joel was lying on his bed, with the covers pulled up conspicuously to his chin. His eyes grew to the size of saucers when he saw me enter his room. I asked him to sit up and chat with me. He swung his fully dressed legs over the side of the bed and sat up. He had fully dressed himself and was prepared for school. I knew what was going on with Joel was not a rational choice. He wasn't simply choosing not to go to school that day. He was addicted to his devices and craved the dopamine they provided. Because of his ADHD and brain injury, he was especially vulnerable to the stimulation the online games provided.

"Hi, Joel. Your mom told me you don't want to go to school today and would rather stay home and play video games." Joel looked down at his hands and mumbled a response. I could see Joel's inner turmoil and conflict as he struggled to articulate his thoughts and feelings.

"Joel, you need to go to school today, and your mom needs to go to work, so I'm going to help you. Today is Wednesday. I will hold on to your tablet and the power cord to your computer." Joel looked up at me, and his eyes widened even more when I reached behind his computer and detached the power cord from the back of his computer and the wall.

"If you go to school today and every day this week, I'll return them on Friday after school." Defeated, Joel slid out of bed slowly, slipped on his shoes, and followed me out of his room. I followed closely behind Sarah and Joel as they drove to the school. I walked Joel into the front office and got him a late pass. As we walked to Joel's classroom, I couldn't help but think about screen time and how it affected his academic and social development, overall well-being, and relationship with his mother. Before Joel entered his class, I turned to him and said, "Joel, I know this is hard for you. I'm proud of you for coming to school today." Joel looked down and nodded. "I also need you to promise me you won't put your hands on your mom like you did last night again." Joel looked up at me with embarrassment and shame on his face. He nodded his head and softly replied, "I promise." I could see the weight of his promise on his shoulders as he walked into the classroom. I patted Joel on the back and gave him an encouraging smile before returning to the front office to speak with Sarah. I reassured Sarah that I would work with Joel and help her develop some strategies to regulate his screen time and manage his behavior. Over the next week, we discussed setting up a reward system for Joel to earn screen time and implementing breaks and other daily activities to help him balance his device use. I strongly recommended that she consult with the therapist to tackle Joel's compulsive behavior, implementing behavior intervention strategies to manage screen time and address underlying issues.

This was my first experience helping a parent address their child's excessive screen time, but it would not be the last. Most of my stories about families who struggle with technology in their homes are a version of Sarah and Joel's story.

Perhaps Sarah and Joel's story sounds familiar to you. Maybe you are seeing your child sinking deeper and deeper into their digital world while losing their connection to the real one. You have tried talking about it, but it inevitably turns into a shouting match. You have tried bribery, scolding, and even pleading. You've tried everything. This is not your fault. They have rigged the game against you and your child. The effect this technology has on your child's brain is difficult to break. In the following chapters, you'll see why and how to counter it.

Chapter Two
How We Got Here and the Teen Mental Health Crisis

Apple's launch of the iPhone in 2007 marked one of the most significant technological advancements of the 21st century. At the time, we had no idea of its influence on our daily lives, communication methods, and social structures and the damage it would do to our children's mental health. If we had, we would have thrown it back in Steve Jobs' face.

Before the iPhone, mobile phones served mainly as tools for making calls, sending texts, and, at most, performing basic web browsing. The idea of a single handheld device integrating a phone, music player, camera, and computer was truly a futuristic concept. People typically carried separate gadgets for different functions: flip phones for calling, digital cameras for taking pictures, MP3 players for listening to music, and personal digital assistants (PDAs) for basic productivity tasks. The iPhone revolutionized this by combining all these functionalities into one elegant device.

When Steve Jobs announced the first iPhone, he famously stated, "Apple is going to reinvent the phone." It signified a major shift in how people interacted with technology and each other. It transformed our methods of accessing information, communicating, and engaging with the digital world.

The launch of the App Store in 2008 further revolutionized this device by creating a dynamic ecosystem of third-party applications that addressed nearly every facet of life. From entertainment and productivity to healthcare and education, the iPhone has become an indispensable tool that empowers individuals and industries.

The original iPhone featured a 3.5-inch display, a 2-megapixel camera, and a multi-touch interface. It operated on a custom version of iOS, then known as iPhone OS, and seamlessly integrated an iPod, phone, and internet access point into one device.

The iPhone 4, released on June 24, 2010, was a groundbreaking update. It sported a sleek glass design and a high-resolution retina display. The inclusion of a front-facing camera gave rise to FaceTime and popularized the "selfie," fundamentally changing our interactions with smartphones.

A 2012 Pew Research report on cell phone ownership revealed that in 2011, 77% of American teenagers had a phone, but only 23% owned a smartphone.[1] Consequently, most teens accessed social media via a computer, often using a shared family device, which limited their privacy and access. While laptop computers and high-speed internet became more prevalent during this period, allowing some teens increased online access, it was when smartphones became common among teens that they could be constantly connected, even away from home.

By 2016, a survey by Common Sense Media indicated that 79% of teens and 28% of children aged 8 to 12 owned smartphones. This widespread smartphone adoption led adolescents to spend significantly more time in the digital world. According to a 2015 Common Sense report, teens with social media accounts spent about two hours daily on these platforms, while overall screen media use among teens averaged nearly seven hours per day for leisure activities, including video games and streaming services like Netflix and YouTube.[2]

A 2015 Pew Research report supported these findings, stating that one in four teens was online "almost constantly." By 2022, this figure had nearly doubled to 46%. These high levels of near-constant online presence reflect the profound impact of smartphones on teen behavior and media consumption.[3]

In today's world, smartphones have seamlessly integrated into the fabric of teenage life, serving as portals to social connectivity, information, and entertainment. However, the omnipresence of these devices raises significant concerns regarding their impact on teenagers' physical and mental well-being. In this chapter, we embark on a journey to unravel the multifaceted effects of excessive phone use on adolescents and delve into the underlying mechanisms that shape their behaviors and attitudes toward technology.

The Adolescent Mental Health Crisis

Our young people's mental health is collapsing. We have reached a point where we can no longer ignore it. It is a full-fledged crisis. The radical shift in our children's mental health outcomes requires a radical response. Before I can suggest how we turn around our children's collapsing mental health, we need to understand how we got here.

We are witnessing a troubling increase in mental health disorders among young people, particularly those related to anxiety and depression. According to the DSM-5-TR, anxiety and depression fall under the psychiatric category known as internalizing disorders. These disorders are characterized by inwardly felt distress, where individuals experience intense emotions such as anxiety, fear, sadness, and hopelessness. They tend to ruminate and often withdraw from social interactions.[4]

Conversely, externalizing disorders involve distress that manifests outwardly, affecting others. These disorders include conduct disorder, difficulties with anger management, and a propensity for violence and risky behavior.[5] Research shows that, across various ages, cultures, and countries, girls and women are more prone to internalizing disorders, while boys and men are more likely to suffer from externalizing disorders.[6] However, it is important to note that both genders can experience both types of disorders.

Anxiety and fear are related but distinct concepts. According to the DSM-5-TR, fear is defined as "the emotional response to a real or perceived imminent threat," while anxiety is "the anticipation of future threat."[7] Both can be appropriate responses to certain situations, but when they become excessive, they can lead to disorders.

You can see in Figure 1.1, the radical upswing of anxiety since 2010. Before 2010, there was very little change in the levels of anxiety in this age group leading up to 2010. In 2012, when the majority of teens had smartphones, there was a rapid and continuing rise in reported anxiety. Anxiety and related disorders continue to be prevalent among young people today. A 2022 study of over 37,000 high school students in Wisconsin reported that the

Percent Anxiety Prevalence, U.S. Young Adults (18-25)

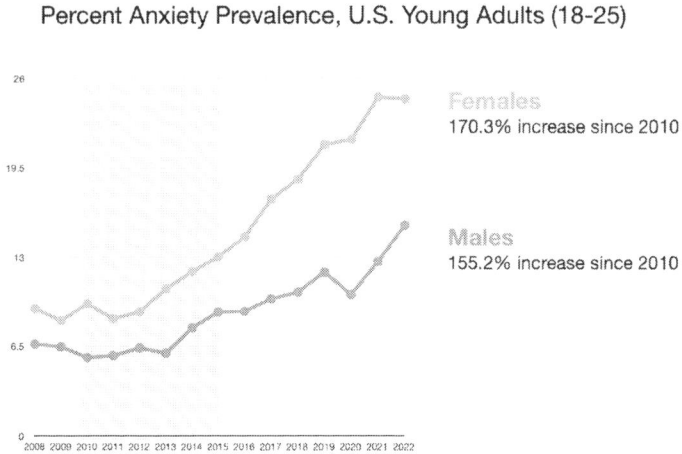

Females
170.3% increase since 2010

Males
155.2% increase since 2010

Figure 1.1 Percent of U.S. young adults (ages 18-15) reporting high levels of anxiety. Feeling Nervous "Most of The Time" or "All of The Time" in Past Month. SOURCE: U.S. National Survey on Drug Use and Health

prevalence of anxiety rose from 34% in 2012 to 44% in 2018, with significant increases among girls and LGBTQ teens.[8]

Anxiety manifests in both the mind and body. Physically, it can cause tension, tightness, and discomfort in the abdomen and chest. Emotionally, it is experienced as dread and worry, often leading to exhaustion.[9] Cognitively, anxiety can impair clear thinking, leading to unproductive rumination and cognitive distortions such as catastrophizing, overgeneralizing, and black-and-white thinking.[10] These distorted thinking patterns, targeted in cognitive behavioral therapy (CBT), often lead to physical symptoms, creating a cycle of anxiety.

Depression is the second most common psychological disorder among young people today. It is characterized by two primary symptoms: a depressed mood (feeling sad, empty, hopeless) and a loss of interest or pleasure in most activities. For a diagnosis of Major Depressive Disorder, these symptoms must be present for at least two weeks. Depression often includes physical symptoms like significant weight loss or gain, changes in sleep patterns, and fatigue. It also involves disordered thinking, including difficulty concentrating, dwelling on personal failings (leading to feelings of guilt), and cognitive distortions similar to those in anxiety. Those experiencing depression may also have suicidal thoughts, as they may feel that their suffering is endless and that death offers an escape.[11]

When did the mental health collapse begin? In 2010. The mental health collapse was primarily seen in the cohort of teens now identified as Generation Z (children born between 1997 and 2012), but not so in older generations who had access to the same technology. Not only was Gen Z in the United States experiencing the same mental health decline, but in other countries, too. This is not a uniquely American experience but a global human experience. 2010 was the jumping-off point of "The Great Rewiring" of our children's brains, as coined by Johnathan Haight in his excellent book, The Anxious Generation.

As you can see in Figure 1.2, before 2010, there was no evidence of a pending adolescent mental health crisis. Self-reporting anxiety and depression for teenagers was relatively flat. Then, in 2012, we saw a sudden and significant increase in major depressive episodes. As we will see, phones and social media disproportionately affect girls. The rise in depression rates was significantly more pronounced for girls than for boys in absolute terms (the number of additional cases since 2010), showing a more pronounced rise. However, since boys started at a lower baseline, the relative increase (percent change since 2010) was similar for both sexes— about 150%. In other words, the prevalence of depression roughly

Major Depression Among Teens (12-17)

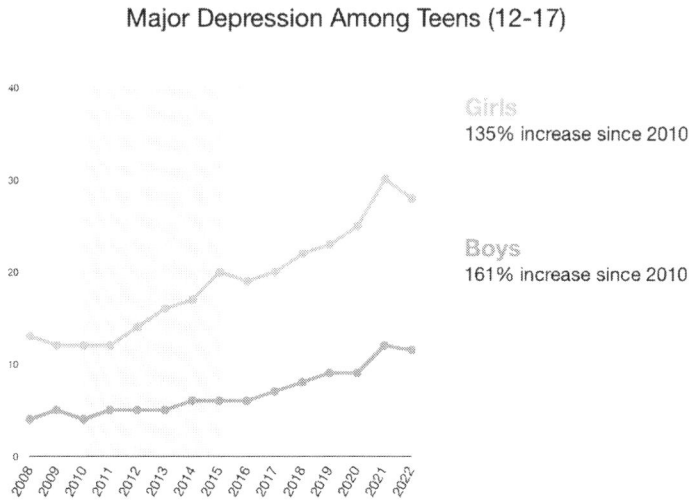

Figure 1.2 SOURCE: U.S. National Survey on Drug Use and Health

doubled and a half for both genders. This rise occurred across all races and social classes.

Those who argue that COVID lockdowns are the sole cause for the teen mental health implosion (COVID did have a profound impact on school-aged children's learning and mental health) cannot explain away the data collected in 2020, which spanned both before and after COVID shutdowns. It revealed that one in four American teen girls had experienced a major depressive episode in the previous year. The data for 2021 showed a steeper increase, indicating that the situation worsened after 2020. However, most of the rise in depression rates occurred before the COVID-19 pandemic.

Self-Harm

As a brand new School Resource Officer, I was quickly introduced to and educated about a growing and very concerning

Emergency Dept Visits for Nonfatal Self-Harm, U.S Teens (Ages 10-14)

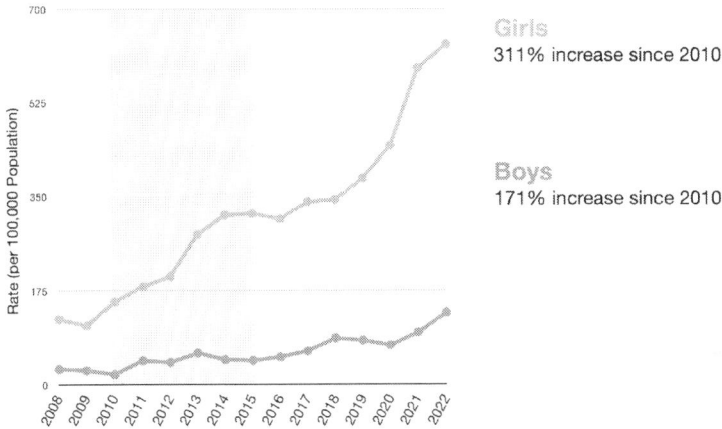

Figure 1.3 SOURCE: Centers for Disease Control and Prevention, National Center for Injury Prevention and Control

externalizing disorder, Non-Suicidal Self Injury, or NSSI. Among teens, this is commonly known as "cutting." The DSM-5 defines NSSI as the "deliberate, self-inflicted destruction of body tissue without suicidal intent and for purposes not socially sanctioned, includes behaviors such as cutting, burning, biting and scratching skin."[12] In both adolescents and adults, rates of NSSI are highest among people who report characteristics associated with emotional distress, such as negative emotionality, depression, anxiety, and emotion dysregulation. NSSI is especially common in people prone to self-directed negative emotions and self-criticism.
[13]

From 2010 to 2020, self-harm rates among young adolescent girls tripled. The rate doubled for older girls aged 15 to 19, whereas for women over 24, it decreased. This suggests that the early 2010s had a particularly severe impact on preteen and young teen girls.

Figure 1.3 highlights intentional self-harm behaviors, including nonfatal suicide attempts and non-suicidal self-injury (NSSI), such as cutting. Nonfatal suicide attempts signal extreme distress and hopelessness, while NSSI is often used as a coping mechanism to handle severe anxiety and depression, particularly among girls and young women.[14] Understanding these patterns is critical to addressing the mental health challenges faced by these groups.

The long-lasting physical and psychological damage NSSI has on a teen and their whole family is devastating. Our schools had a confidential phone number students could use to text a tip. Those tips came to me, the assistant principal, and the school counselor. One morning, I received a screenshot of an Instagram account belonging to one of my seventh-grade students through our student text tip line. Let's call her Jenny. Jenny had fifty followers of students at the school, and for the past month, Jenny had been talking about her emotions, including her extreme anxiety and feelings of physical inadequacy. The evening before the tip, she posted a graphic image of her forearm.

The Instagram image revealed a row of bloody wounds running down the length of her inner arm. Jenny was called into the office to speak to the counselor and me. The next call was to her mother, who rushed to the school. We talked to the mother alone, explaining everything we knew up to that point. As the tears welled in her eyes, she said, "Jenny wears long-sleeved shirts every day ... I didn't know." We brought Mom and Jenny together in the counselor's office. Mom ran to her daughter, wrapped her arms around Jenny, and held her for a long time. Jenny then pulled back the sleeves of her shirt, revealing the damage. Fresh wounds were laying over healed scars. This had been going on for months. I will never forget the sound that emanated from Jenny's mom's throat.

It began as a gasp and then a soul-crushing moan of sadness and despair. I heard the counselor sob next to me. Everyone in the room, including me, was heartbroken for this mother and her daughter.

I spoke to Jenny's mom on and off the following year. She shared with me the anxiety and depression she was dealing with after learning about Jenny's self-harm and depression. She carried crushing guilt for not knowing and protecting her daughter. This guilt was only compounded by the realization that Jenny had been talking about her feelings for months on Instagram. If she had only looked at her Instagram for a moment, she would have seen Jenny's path and could have helped her months before our tragic meeting in the counselor's office.

Teen Suicide

An alarming trend has emerged among adolescents nationwide: escalating suicide rates, with a disproportionate impact on youth of color and LGBTQ+ youth. This phenomenon is unfolding against a backdrop of pervasive feelings of hopelessness, sadness, loneliness, and suicidal ideation reported by teenagers. According to a report by the Centers for Disease Control and Prevention (CDC), which analyzed mental health and suicidal behaviors from 2011 to 2021, 13% of high school girls had attempted suicide, with 30% having seriously contemplated it. These figures are even more stark among LGBTQ+ teens, where the rate of attempted suicides exceeds 20%, and nearly 45% have seriously considered taking their own lives.[15]

Between 2000 and 2018, the suicide rate among youth aged 10 to 24 escalated precipitously from 6.8 to 10.7 per 100,000, as evidenced by death certificate data.[16] This disturbing trend propelled suicide to the second leading cause of death for the 10 to 14 age bracket by 2021, according to the CDC (Facts About Suicide, May 2023). Following a decline in the overall suicide rate in 2019 and 2020, the figures rebounded close to the 2018 peak in 2021.[17]

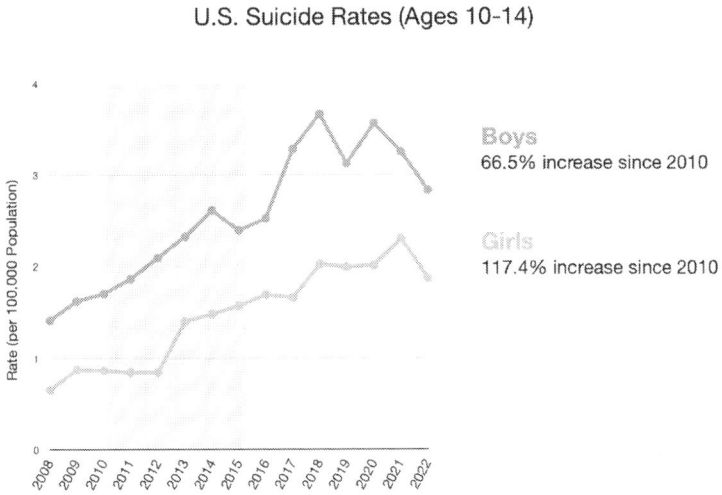

Figure 1.4 SOURCE: CDC Wisqars Fatal Injury Reports

Figure 1.4 reveals a troubling trend—the suicide rate among young adolescent girls, which had fluctuated within a narrow band since the 1980s, began its ominous ascent in 2008. A particularly alarming spike occurred in 2012, breaking the prior stability. Between 2010 and 2021, this rate didn't just climb—it skyrocketed to an astonishing 167%.

"We focus so much on symptom reduction at the individual level, but without really contextualizing these forces that are more systemic," said Jocelyn Meza, PhD, a clinical psychologist and professor in psychiatry at the University of California, Los Angeles, who studies culturally responsive interventions for underrepresented youth. "We're really ignoring social structures in our treatment development." More than 20% of teens have seriously considered suicide. Psychologists and communities can help tackle the problem.[18] I agree with Dr. Meza's assessment. We should be asking, what changed for preteen and younger teen girls in the early 2010s when the years leading up to 2010 were relatively flat concerning teen suicide rates? As shown in the above graph, girls were hit the hardest.

A lot may have to do with how they see themselves and what the world (faceless people on Instagram) has to say about how they look. In June 2010, the iPhone 4 was introduced, featuring the first front-facing camera, revolutionizing how people took selfies. Additionally, 2010 saw the launch of Instagram. Instagram remained relatively niche until Facebook acquired it in 2012, propelling its user base from 10 million in late 2011 to 90 million by early 2013. This marked the beginning of the smartphone and selfie-centric social media landscape we recognize today. By 2012, many teenage girls felt pressured to keep up with the trend of owning a smartphone and an Instagram account, leading to constant self-comparison.

Over the subsequent years, social media became even more captivating with the introduction of advanced filters and editing software on Instagram. It was like an arms race of who could get the most likes by using filters and apps like Facetune to create a perfect image of themselves. This technological shift caused girls to see their reflections as less appealing than the edited images they viewed online.[19] Take a moment and think about this. Your daughter does not think her natural face is good enough. They believe that they have to use an app to doctor their photos, creating an untrue representation of themselves, just to be accepted by others. Little girls as young as six years old are buying skin care products to make their already perfect skin look better.[20] Something very sad and disturbing is happening to our girls' perception of themselves and how they gauge their self-worth.

While girls gravitated toward social media, boys were drawn into digital activities such as immersive online multiplayer video games, YouTube, Reddit, and easily accessible online pornography. We will explore the power these online experiences have on our boys and, to a smaller extent, our girls, as well as examine the neurological pathways that make them addictive.

The proliferation of smartphones and social media among teenagers has reshaped how they interact with the world around them. Smartphones offer unparalleled convenience and connectivity, from instant communication through social media platforms to immersive gaming experiences and unlimited access to information. However, this constant connectivity comes at a cost. These experiences have begun to replace real face-to-face experiences and are now available every day on a device they can carry in their pocket. We purchased these devices for our children, not knowing what the actual cost was for our children's mental health and happiness. I wonder how our choices would have been different if, in 2007, Steve Jobs had held up the first iPhone and said, "This device will change everything. You will be able to communicate in ways you never thought possible. It will change the world. It will also more than double teen anxiety and depression, triple the number of girls hurting themselves, and more than double teen suicidal ideation. But you can listen to music and play games, too!" Would any parent buy it for their child? We just didn't know. The good news is it doesn't have to remain like this.

We can turn the ship around and work to get our children's mental health heading back in the right direction.

Chapter Three
Dopamine – Our Brains are Making This Hard

Why is getting our children to put down the game controller or their phone so difficult? Why are these devices so addictive? It's because of dopamine. Dopamine is mainly recognized for its role in reward and behavior reinforcement because it's the key neurotransmitter in our brain's reward system. It releases dopamine in the brain to drive feelings of achievement, success, pleasure, and satisfaction. Dopamine also plays a role in shaping behavior. When dopamine is released, we experience pleasure, which motivates us to repeat the actions that caused it.[21]

Historically, foods high in calories have been linked to survival. When something boosts our chances of survival, we evolve to enjoy it. What we call "pleasure" is our brain guiding us, saying, "Do more of this; it's good for us." Because this action benefits us, we crave it again. When we eat a doughnut, dopamine is released, giving us pleasure and reinforcing the behavior. If eating calorie-rich food brings pleasure, we seek it out again—this is what we know as anticipation. Dopamine controls pleasure, reinforcement, and anticipation; this feedback loop evolved to help us survive. This explains why obesity is a common issue. Many foods today contain sugar at unnatural levels. These foods flood our brains with dopamine, creating a hard-to-break feedback loop.[22]

Video games and social media can also hijack the dopamine system. Designers of games and social media have learned how to control our dopamine response, giving us pleasure, reinforcement, and anticipation without helping us survive. Sean Parker, the creator of Napster and co-founder of Facebook, explained how the game is rigged against us:[23]

> You know ... the thought process that went into building these applications, Facebook being the first of them to ... consume as much of your time and conscious attention as possible. And that means that we need to sort of give you a little dopamine hit every once in a while. Um, because someone liked or commented on a photo or a post or what-ever, and that's going to get you to contribute more content, and that's going to get you, you know, more likes and comments. I mean, it's a, it's a social validation feedback loop that ... it's exactly the kind of thing ... a hacker like myself would come up with because you're exploiting a vulnera-bility in, in human psychology. And I just, I, I think that we, you know, we, the inventors, creators ... understood this consciously, and we did it anyway.

Game designers are exceptionally skilled at maximizing dopamine release in the brain. They know players get bored and quit if a game is too easy. They'll give up if it's too hard because the dopamine release isn't worth the effort. So, they fine-tune the difficulty to maximize dopamine release, reinforcing the behavior and increasing anticipation.[24]

Dopamine circuits can develop tolerance, the brain's way of keeping things in a "normal" range. When something exceeds that range, the brain adjusts by lowering the signal. It's like turning down the volume on a music player when it's too loud.[25]

In video games, dopamine signals get heightened, causing dopamine receptors to downregulate—turning down the "volume" of the signal. This means that even a lot of dopamine release results in just a normal level of enjoyment. The problem is that when we stop playing video games and try playing a board game, we get a regular dopamine signal, but with fewer receptors, the total "volume" is too low—making a 2-dimensional board game less enjoyable. The brain becomes less able to enjoy lower stimulating activities like board games or reading a book after too much gaming.

Have you noticed that when your child starts gaming, they have fun in the first hour? But after four hours of playing, they're no longer enjoying themselves—they're like zombies, no longer smiling, laughing, or talking. Plus, whenever you try to get them to do something other than gaming, they feel bored and resist it with all their might. This happens because of dopamine tolerance—if they've been playing games for hours, it takes time for them to get used to enjoying other activities.

Research shows that video games suppress the brain's emotional circuits. Gaming essentially shuts down the amygdala, which is the area of the brain where negative emotions come from, giving temporary relief from daily stress. This isn't unique to gaming.

After a tough day, going to a bar for a drink or watching TV can also help relieve stress by suppressing negative emotions.[26]

However, any activity that successfully suppresses negative emotions has the potential to be addictive. If we're feeling bad, stressed, ashamed, or scared, and we find something that temporarily makes those feelings disappear, that activity gets reinforced. The problems fade into the background, and we focus only on what feels good.

This is what happens with video games—brain scans show that when we're feeling fear, anger, frustration, or sadness and then start gaming, the amygdala begins to calm down. Our emotions are suppressed, making gaming a powerful coping mechanism.[27]

The situation worsens when your child relies on video games to manage their emotions. Their ability to handle negative emotions without gaming decreases. As their coping skills shrink, the emotions they've been avoiding by gaming start to show up in other ways. This can lead to temper tantrums, being easily frustrated, or other unusual behaviors like isolation, withdrawal, sarcasm, or cynicism.

In short, when your child seems addicted to gaming, it's not just about a dopamine rush. It's about depending on video games for emotional regulation. The more gaming suppresses the amygdala, the more your child will use it as an escape.

Throughout this program, we will discuss how to talk to your child about their gaming and social media use. The techniques will teach you to work equally well on a child who is excessively gaming or can't live without social media. If you have a child who appears to be addicted to TikTok and we are giving an example about gaming, substitute TikTok for gaming and carry on.

Chapter Four
Starting the Conversation and Disarming Fear

A s parents, we all want what's best for our children, but when it comes to video games or social media, it can feel like we're navigating a minefield.

Communication is the cornerstone of any healthy relationship, especially between parents and teens. When discussing sensitive topics like excessive phone or video game use, or even drug and alcohol use, how you communicate is just as important as what you communicate. One of the most important goals you can set is to have an open, honest conversation with your child about their screen time—one where they feel completely at ease, without the fear that the discussion will end with their console or phone being taken away. This approach minimizes defensiveness and maximizes the chances of a positive outcome.

Self-Reflection

Before initiating the conversation, take some time for self-reflection. Consider your phone habits and how they might influence your teen. Are you modeling the behavior you wish to see in your child? Are you looking at your phone and endlessly scrolling when you should be engaging with your family? Are you using your phone or gaming console as a means of escape and not being honest with your own feelings? Is your technology usage disconnecting you from meaningful experiences with members of your family? Awareness of your usage can help you approach the conversation from a place of empathy and understanding.

Choose the Right Time and Place

Timing is crucial when discussing sensitive topics. Choose a moment when your teen is relaxed and not preoccupied with other tasks. A private setting is ideal, free from distractions and interruptions. This ensures that you and your teen can focus entirely on the conversation. Many of the important talks I had with my boys were driving somewhere. I would ask my son if he wanted to go out for ice cream with me. "Yes," was the only answer to that question. On the drive or at a table enjoying a dessert, I had the opportunity to have a conversation with my child without distractions in an unthreatening environment.

Removing the Pressure: It's Not a Battle

Too often, these conversations feel like a battle or a contest where the prize is how much screen time your child will be allowed. If you want to truly engage your child and have a meaningful dialogue, the first step is to remove that "prize" from the equation. You need to create an environment where your child knows that nothing they say will directly influence how much gaming time they're allowed. This is crucial for building trust and opening up a line of communication.

Setting the Stage: A Nonjudgmental Conversation

Being upfront with your child is essential to starting this non-judgmental conversation. You might say, "Nothing you tell me right now will affect your screen time. There may be conversations about that in the future, and I'd love for you to be part of the process when we get there, but this conversation has nothing to do with that. My only goal right now is to understand."

By setting this clear boundary, you're telling your child that this conversation isn't about punishment or restriction—it's about understanding them and what's important to them. This approach eases their anxiety and opens the door to a more honest and open discussion. To reduce your child's fear of losing something they cherish, like gaming, try starting the conversation with these approaches:

Express Curiosity:

"I'd like to sit down and talk to you about how much you play video games because I want to understand it better."

Share Your Perspective:

"When I see video games, they seem recreational to me. I know you've enjoyed other fun activities, so it's confusing that you're so into gaming now. I haven't seen you get this absorbed in something before."

Understand Their World:

In your initial conversation, emphasize that you genuinely want to understand why games are so important to them. Ask them what they enjoy about gaming and what it means to them. If you've been judgmental in the past, acknowledge that and apologize. Owning up to your mistakes can significantly improve your relationship. For example, you might say:

"I've been worried about your gaming for a while, and I'm sure you've noticed. In the past, I've let my fear for you shape how I've acted, and I've been harsh about setting limits. But I haven't really tried to understand why you play video games, what you enjoy about them, and what it's like to be a kid today. I'm sorry for that, and I want to learn more. I'm still concerned about some of your behaviors, but I think we need to understand each other better to move forward. While we're talking, I'm not planning to change any gaming limits. How would you feel about helping me understand the gaming world better?"

Chapter Five
Negotiation Strategies

As a crisis negotiator, my goal was to build rapport with a person with whom I had no previous connection. I met them for the first time on the worst day of their lives, and I may not have anything in common with them. When we could help that person walk outside and surrender to the police, they almost always said, "I just wanted someone to listen to me." The strategies I will teach you are the exact ones I used to make a connection with a person in crisis. You might agree that talking to a kid about their screen time might feel like a hostage negotiation.

Once you have started the nonjudgmental conversation we covered in Chapter 4, we need to continue it and do three things: understand your child's digital world, build rapport with them, and meet them where they are. Ultimately, we want to recruit our children to our side. We want them to work with us, not against us, regulating their screen time.

I will share a variety of communication techniques for engaging with your child, which may feel overwhelming at first. Instead of trying to implement everything at once, start with one or two negotiation techniques that resonate with you. This approach lets you gain confidence and see how these methods work in real conversations with your child. As you become more comfortable, you can gradually introduce one or two more techniques, building your communication skills step-by-step.

Technique #1: The Open-Ended Question Strategy

The Open-Ended Question communication strategy is a powerful tool for connecting with teenagers in a way that feels safe and supportive for them. Inviting dialogue rather than dictating terms allows teenagers to express themselves openly and honestly, leading to more meaningful and productive conversations. Whether you're discussing hobbies, relationships, or sensitive topics, open-ended questions can help you build trust, understand your teenager's perspective, and ultimately, guide them more effectively through the challenges of adolescence.

Understanding the Open-Ended Question Strategy

Open-ended questions encourage discussion rather than elicit a simple yes or no answer. Unlike closed-ended questions, which can often feel like interrogations, open-ended questions give teenagers the freedom to express themselves in their own words. This approach empowers them by validating their opinions and provides valuable insights into their world—insights that might otherwise remain hidden.

For example, instead of asking, "Do you play video games too much?"—a question that might make a teenager feel defensive—you could ask, "What do you enjoy about gaming?" This subtle shift in phrasing opens the door to a conversation where the teenager feels safe to explore and explain their interests. It also positions you as a curious and supportive listener rather than an authority figure passing judgment.

The Power of Open-Ended Questions in Teenage Communication

The Open-Ended Question strategy is particularly effective because it reduces the likelihood of defensiveness and promotes a more relaxed, open conversation. Like all individuals, teenagers are more willing to share their thoughts and feelings when they don't feel threatened or judged. By asking questions that focus on understanding rather than evaluating, you create a space where they can talk freely.

This strategy is also versatile, making it applicable in various scenarios—from discussing hobbies like gaming to addressing more sensitive issues like peer pressure or substance use. For instance, rather than asking directly, "Do you drink alcohol?"—which might provoke a defensive response—you could ask, "Does anyone at your school drink alcohol?" This question opens up the conversation without being accusatory, allowing the teenager to express their thoughts and experiences more comfortably.

Examples of Effective Open-Ended Questions

To effectively use the Open-Ended Question strategy, it's important to ask questions that are neutral and nonjudgmental. Here are some examples tailored to different contexts:

Gaming/Social Media-Related Questions:

- "What do you enjoy about video games?"

- "What's your favorite kind of video game?"

- "What's your favorite type of video to watch on TikTok?"

- "I saw you practicing dance moves. Was that for a video on social media?"

- "Do your friends play games too? What's that like?"

Sensitive Topics:

- "Do any of your friends struggle with gaming too much? What's that like for them?"

- "If you ever struggled with gaming, would you feel comfortable telling us? What could we do to help you feel more relaxed?"

- "How does it feel if you don't get a lot of likes on a video or image you took so much time to get right?"

- "What do your friends think about marijuana or vaping? How do those conversations go?"

These questions invite teenagers to share their thoughts and help you understand their motivations, social dynamics, and potential challenges they might be facing. By starting with broad, open-ended questions, you create a foundation of trust and understanding that can lead to deeper, more meaningful conversations over time.

Validating and Extending the Conversation

Once a teenager responds to an open-ended question, validating their feelings and thoughts is crucial before moving the conversation forward. For example, if your child responds to a question about gaming by saying, "Gaming is fun. All of my friends do it. It's not a big deal. This is how we hang out," you might say, "I hear you. When I was your age, I only wanted to hang out with my friends. I'm curious—what makes video games such a good way to hang out?"

This response shows that you're listening and that you respect their viewpoint. It also gently encourages them to explore their feelings and experiences without feeling pressured or misunderstood.

Building Better Communication Over Time

Effective use of open-ended questions requires patience and consistency. Don't rush to ask all your questions in one sitting; spread them out over time and let the conversations develop naturally. Building better communication with your teenager is a gradual process, and allowing space for them to open up at their own pace is essential.

As you continue to use open-ended questions, you'll likely find that your teenager becomes more comfortable sharing their thoughts and feelings with you. This strategy helps you gain deeper insights into their world and strengthens your relationship by promoting a sense of mutual respect and understanding.

Technique #2: Reflective Listening for Emotional Validation

Reflective listening is a powerful strategy for validating your teenager's emotions and creating a deeper connection. While it may require practice and patience, the rewards are well worth the effort. By resisting the urge to immediately fix or judge and instead focusing on reflecting back on your child's feelings, you create a safe space for them to express themselves openly. This approach enhances communication and strengthens the emotional bond between you and your child, making it easier to navigate challenging topics like gaming, social media, and beyond. Through reflective listening, you show your child that their feelings matter and that you are genuinely there to support and understand them.

Understanding Reflective Listening

Reflective listening involves echoing back what your child has said, not as a question, but as a statement that reflects their emotions and experiences. This technique effectively validates your child's feelings without introducing judgment or solutions too quickly. By simply acknowledging what your child has shared, you create a safe space for them to express themselves more fully.

For example, consider a scenario where your daughter comes to you upset after posting a photo on social media:

Your Daughter: "Mom, I posted an image on Instagram, and people are saying I'm fat. Everyone hates me. I don't like the way I look!"

You: Instinctive Response (incorrect): "No, you're beautiful. I love you so much."

You: Reflective Listening (correct): "I hear that you're feeling unattractive and that people dislike you. You must feel isolated and hurt."

In the instinctive response, although well-meaning, you inadvertently dismiss your daughter's feelings by trying to counter them. On the other hand, reflective listening validates her emotions, showing that you understand her pain without trying to fix it immediately. This validation can make her feel seen and heard, encouraging her to continue sharing her thoughts and emotions.

Why Reflective Listening is Challenging

Reflective listening goes against our natural instincts, especially when our child is distressed. The desire to protect, reassure, or solve problems is strong, but these responses can sometimes shut down communication. When we jump too quickly to fix a situation, we may inadvertently signal to our child that their feelings are wrong or that they should not feel like they do.

Instead, reflective listening requires us to pause, listen fully, and reflect back on what our child has said. This approach might initially feel counterintuitive, especially when you want to comfort your child or correct a misconception. However, practicing restraint and focusing on reflection allows your child to explore their emotions more deeply, which often leads to a more productive and meaningful conversation.

Applying Reflective Listening in Everyday Conversations

Reflective listening can be integrated into daily interactions with your teenager, particularly when discussing important or sensitive topics. Let's apply this strategy to a conversation about gaming:

You: "What do you enjoy about video games?"

Child: "I love playing games and want to play games all day long."

You: Instinctive Response (incorrect): "Well, I think that's bad for you."

You: Reflective Listening (correct): "Hmm, it sounds like all you want to do is play video games."

In this example, the instinctive response might create an oppositional dynamic, where the conversation becomes a debate rather than a dialogue. Reflective listening, however, mirrors what your child has said, giving them no reason to become defensive. This often leads to them sharing more:

Child: "I like playing video games because I think school is boring."

You: "Hmm. Sounds like school is really boring to you, and you find games more intellectually challenging. Is that right?"

This continuation deepens your understanding of your child's motivations and shows them that you are genuinely interested in their perspective. Reflective listening encourages them to explore and express their feelings more openly without fearing being judged or misunderstood.

The Benefits of Emotional Validation

Validating your child's emotions through reflective listening can have profound effects on your relationship. When children feel understood and supported, their emotional defenses lower, reducing feelings of threat or conflict. This emotional validation helps calm the amygdala, the brain's fear center, making it easier for them to engage in a constructive conversation.

Over time, practicing reflective listening builds trust and strengthens the bond between you and your child. They begin to see you as an authority figure and a supportive ally who truly understands them. This shift in perception can lead to more open communication and a greater willingness on their part to listen to your guidance.

Technique #3: Expressing Confusion

Communicating with teenagers can often feel like walking a tightrope. Direct confrontations can lead to defensiveness, while avoiding difficult conversations can allow problematic behaviors or misconceptions to go unchallenged. The "Expressing Confusion" communication strategy offers a subtle, nonconfrontational way to address statements that don't make sense or are simply wrong. By expressing genuine confusion, you invite your teenager to clarify their reasoning, gently highlighting any flaws in their logic without making them feel attacked. This approach can turn potential conflicts into constructive conversations, allowing for a more open and reflective dialogue.

Understanding the Expressing Confusion Strategy

The Expressing Confusion strategy is akin to verbal jiu-jitsu. Rather than directly confronting or correcting your teenager's statements, you express confusion in a way that encourages them to explain their reasoning. This technique disarms defensiveness by avoiding outright opposition and instead frames the conversation as a collaborative effort to understand their perspective.

Imagine a scenario where you receive an email from your child's teacher expressing concern about their performance in class. You decide to discuss this with your child:

You: "Your teacher sent me an email today saying you are not doing as well as you should be on your assignments. She said you seem very tired and disengaged. She asked you why you were so tired, and you said it was because you were up late playing video games."

Child: "It's not a big deal. I'm still passing."

At this point, rather than confronting the issue head-on, you might first use reflective listening to acknowledge their feelings:

You: "You feel like it's not a big deal because you're still passing."

Next, you could ask an open-ended question to explore their perspective further:

You: "Do you feel your grades reflect your intellect?"

Child: "No, I could get better grades if I wanted. I'll make it up later."

Here's where the "Expressing Confusion" strategy comes into play. Rather than challenging their statement directly, you express confusion, signaling that you don't fully understand their logic:

You: "I'm a little confused. You're gaming on school nights, not going to class prepared, and not getting good grades, yet you're saying everything's fine. How will you get into college if you're not doing well in school? Maybe I don't understand your plan. Can you help me better understand it?"

By framing your response as confusion rather than criticism, you allow your teenager to clarify their thinking. This subtle approach will enable them to confront the inconsistencies in their reasoning on their own terms, reducing the likelihood of defensiveness.

Why the Expressing Confusion Strategy Works

Teenagers often use defensive tactics when they know their reasoning is flawed but are unwilling to admit it. Direct challenges to their logic can lead to arguments or shutdowns, where they stop engaging in the conversation altogether. The Expressing Confusion strategy works because it avoids triggering this defensiveness. By positioning yourself as someone simply trying to understand, you reduce the perceived threat and encourage them to keep talking.

This technique also subtly shifts the burden of proof onto the teenager. When you express confusion, you're not stating that they're wrong; you're asking them to explain how they're right. This often leads them to realize the gaps in their own logic, which can be more effective than having those gaps pointed out by someone else.

Also, you should maintain a supportive and nonjudgmental tone by avoiding accusations or direct confrontation. This approach advances a more open and trusting relationship, making it easier for your teenager to share their thoughts and feelings with you in the future.

Applying the Strategy in Everyday Conversations

The Expressing Confusion strategy can be used in a wide range of situations where a teenager's statements or actions don't align with reality or with their own goals. Here's how it might look in a different context:

Scenario: Your child spends excessive time on video games and neglects their schoolwork.

You: "I noticed you've been playing a lot of video games lately, and your grades have slipped. You said you wanted to go to college, but gaming seems to take up most of your time."

Child: "It's fine. I'll get my grades up later."

You: "I'm a little confused. You're spending a lot of time gaming, and your grades are slipping, but you're confident everything will be fine. Can you help me understand how that's going to work?"

In this scenario, the child is prompted to explain their plan or realize they might not have one. This realization is more likely to lead to constructive action than if you had told them their approach was flawed.

Key Takeaway

The Expressing Confusion strategy aims not to trap your teenager in their own logic but to encourage them to think more deeply about their choices. By presenting yourself as genuinely confused rather than confrontational, you invite them to engage in a dialogue where they feel safe to explore and, if necessary, reassess their reasoning.

This technique disarms defensiveness, making it easier for your teenager to hear what you are saying and consider an alternative point of view. As long as they're talking, they're also listening, which is crucial for effective communication. Over time, this strategy can help you build a stronger, more open relationship with your teenager, where challenging conversations become opportunities for growth rather than sources of conflict.

By expressing confusion rather than confrontation, you subtly guide your teenager toward recognizing the inconsistencies in their logic while maintaining a supportive and nonjudgmental tone. This approach enhances communication and encourages teenagers to think critically about their decisions and their impact on their future.

Overcoming Objections

Overcoming objections to reducing screen time isn't about battling against your child's love for video games; it's about helping them discover and nurture real-world interests that can provide similar or even greater satisfaction. By engaging in open-ended conversations and exploring their emotions and interests, you can guide them toward finding activities that offer the same sense of agency and fulfillment as gaming. This approach reduces their reliance on screens and helps them build a life full of diverse experiences and meaningful accomplishments. You can help your child find balance and purpose in the real world through patience, understanding, and collaboration.

Understanding the Appeal of Gaming

To effectively address your child's screen time, it's essential to understand why gaming is so enticing. Video games provide an immediate sense of achievement, clear goals, and a structured environment where success is rewarded. This can be incredibly seductive for teenagers, who may feel powerless in other areas of their lives. The virtual world offers a place where they can excel, make decisions, and see the direct results of their actions.

Given this powerful draw, simply telling your child to spend less time gaming is unlikely to be effective. They may perceive it as losing the one area where they feel competent and in control. Instead, the conversation needs to focus on helping them understand the broader impact of their gaming habits and exploring other avenues that can provide similar satisfaction.

The Challenge of Overcoming Objections

When you broach the topic of screen time with your child, you may encounter strong objections. They might argue that gaming is harmless, that it's how they unwind, or that they don't have any other interests. It's important to acknowledge these feelings and not dismiss them outright. Overcoming these objections isn't about forcing them to give up gaming through sheer willpower; it's about helping them find a compelling reason to balance gaming with other activities that enrich their lives.

Engaging in Open-Ended Conversations

One effective strategy is to engage your child in open-ended conversations, encouraging them to reflect on their gaming habits and explore other interests. Instead of providing all the answers, use open-ended questions to guide the discussion. This approach allows them to consider their thoughts and feelings, making them more invested in the outcome.

For example, you might start by asking, "What is it like to have almost no outside interests besides gaming?" This question isn't accusatory; it invites your child to think about their life beyond the screen. Their response could offer valuable insights into what might be missing in their life and what needs gaming is fulfilling.

Other questions to consider might include:

- "What do you think is cool?"

- "What excites you?"

- "If you could change one thing about the world, what would it be?"

These questions are designed to spark curiosity and self-reflection. They're not about pointing out the negatives of gaming but about helping your child explore what else might interest them. The goal is to identify what feelings or experiences gaming provides that might also be found in real-world activities.

Helping Your Child Discover New Interests

Once you've tapped into your child's interests and emotions, work with them to explore how they can get more involved in those areas. If they're passionate about something but unsure how to pursue it, offer to brainstorm ideas together. For instance, if they're interested in creativity, you might suggest art classes, coding workshops, or even starting a blog. If they're drawn to adventure, outdoor activities like hiking or rock climbing could be appealing.

It's important to approach this process collaboratively rather than dictating what they should do. By involving them in the decision-making process, you empower them to take ownership of their choices, making them more likely to engage in new activities.

Shifting the Focus from Virtual to Real-World Fulfillment

These conversations aim to help your child see that the real world isn't a place where they're powerless or without agency. Like in video games, the real world offers opportunities for them to make a meaningful difference, achieve goals, and experience a sense of accomplishment. The more you engage them in discussions about their passions and interests, the more they'll begin seeing the potential for fulfillment outside the virtual world.

By guiding your child through this process, you're not just helping them reduce screen time—you're helping them build a richer, more balanced life. The transition from the virtual world to the real world isn't about giving up what they love; it's about expanding their horizons and finding new ways to experience joy, purpose, and success.

Chapter Six

Taking the Next Step: Sharing Your Point of View

When creating screen time boundaries with your child, how you communicate your perspective is crucial to ensuring a successful and cooperative outcome. It's important not to rush into sharing your point of view before your child feels honestly heard and understood. Establishing a solid foundation of trust and open communication will pave the way for a more productive and empathetic discussion about screen time limits.

1. Express Gratitude for Their Engagement

Once your child has begun to engage in the conversation and open up to you, it's essential to acknowledge and express gratitude for their effort. Discussing difficult topics like screen time boundaries can be challenging, and your child's willingness to participate is a significant step forward.

Start by thanking them for their engagement and highlighting that you've listened carefully to their concerns and interests. This acknowledgment helps reinforce that you value their input and are genuinely interested in understanding their perspective. Here's how you might phrase it:

"Hey, thank you. I really appreciate that we've been talking over the last month. I've been trying to learn from you, and I feel like I understand this stuff much better now. I understand you want to play games because they help you connect with your friends and relax. Is that right?"

By asking for their confirmation, you create an opportunity for them to feel validated. If you've built a good rapport, it should be difficult for them to say no to a question like this. Once they agree, it signals they're open to hearing your point of view.

2. State Your Objective

After your child has confirmed their understanding, it's time to state your objective clearly. This step involves explaining your ultimate goal: working together to meet both of your needs while reducing conflict over gaming or social media use. Begin by reminding your child that, as their parent, your primary responsibility is to prepare them for real life.

When you present your concerns, balance your own priorities with an acknowledgment of their needs. This approach demonstrates that you're not trying to undermine their interests but to find a harmonious balance.

Example:

"Here's what's important to me: spending quality time as a family without the distraction of phones or gaming devices, keeping your body healthy through sports or exercise, and doing well in school. I know you care about spending time with your friends, and I agree that having a healthy social life is important. My concern is that there's a difference between being on your phone all the time with your friends and having a healthy social life."

This statement clarifies your objectives and shows that you understand and respect their perspective. It's crucial to frame your concerns to align with their interests, making it easier for them to see the value in what you're proposing.

3. Reassure Them That Your Goal Isn't to Take Things Away

Children often interpret attempts to limit their gaming or screen time as a punishment or an effort to take away something they love. It's important to reassure them that this isn't your goal. Instead, explain that past efforts to limit screen time aimed to achieve specific goals, such as ensuring their well-being and development.

Emphasize that you're not trying to deprive them of something they enjoy but are instead focused on finding a balance that supports their growth while allowing them to continue enjoying their hobbies.

Example: "I want you to know that when we've talked about limiting gaming in the past, it wasn't about punishing you. It was about ensuring you're healthy, doing well in school, and spending time with family. My goal isn't to take away something you love but to work together to find a balance."

This reassurance can help alleviate their fears and reduce resistance, making them more willing to collaborate on a plan.

4. Collaborate on a Plan

The final step is to actively involve your child in creating a plan that meets their needs and yours. Express your hope that you can work together to help them meet their basic obligations—such as schoolwork, physical activity, and family time—while minimizing the negative impact of excessive gaming.

Encourage them to contribute ideas and discuss how you can help them achieve a balanced lifestyle without cutting out their current online friendships or interests. It's important to get them to agree verbally that this is a shared goal, as this agreement is critical to their commitment to the plan. Example:

"I know you've mentioned that you're reluctant to limit your social media time or find other real-life activities with your friends. I'm trying to think about how we can help you become more socially comfortable without cutting out your online friends. Do you think we can work together on this?"

By framing the conversation as a collaborative effort, you make it clear that you're on the same team and working toward a common goal. This approach creates a sense of partnership and increases the likelihood of a successful outcome.

Chapter Seven
Techniques to Overcome Objections and Build Cooperation

The communication strategies of Feel-Felt-Found, If... Then ... What If, Simple Swap, and How Will We Know?—are invaluable tools for overcoming objections from teenagers by promoting understanding, collaboration, and critical thinking. These methods address the root of resistance by acknowledging the teenager's perspective, offering balanced alternatives, and involving them in decision-making. By shifting the conversation from conflict to cooperation, these strategies mitigate pushback and encourage teenagers to take ownership of their choices. These specific strategies are used by crisis negotiators all over the world to help navigate challenging discussions and strengthen the trust and respect essential for a cooperative relationship. Each of these strategies provides a framework for opening dialogues and finding solutions that respect both the parent's needs and the teenager's desires.

1. The Feel-Felt-Found Strategy

Connecting with teenagers can be challenging in the complex landscape of adolescent communication. Parents and educators often struggle to find the right balance between guiding and supporting teens without alienating them. The "Feel-Felt-Found" communication strategy offers a powerful and empathetic approach to bridge this gap. This method acknowledges a teenager's feelings and provides a relatable experience and a constructive solution. By leveraging this technique, adults can achieve a more open and trusting relationship with their teens.

Understanding the Feel-Felt-Found Strategy

The Feel-Felt-Found strategy is a three-step communication method designed to validate emotions, share experiences, and gently introduce new perspectives. It is particularly effective when addressing concerns or behaviors that may require adjustment. The core of this approach lies in its ability to connect with teenagers' emotional states, making them feel understood and respected.

1. Feel: The first step is acknowledging and validating the teenager's feelings. This is crucial because teenagers are often in a phase of emotional turbulence, where their feelings may be intense and sometimes confusing even to themselves. By recognizing their emotions, you demonstrate empathy and create a safe space for open communication.

Example: "I understand that gaming helps you relax after a long day."

2. Felt: The second step involves sharing a personal experience or a relatable story. Doing so shows that you have been in a similar situation and that their feelings are normal and understandable.

This helps to build rapport and trust as the teenager sees that you have navigated similar challenges.

Example: "I felt the same way about my hobbies when I was your age."

3. Found: The final step introduces a potential solution or alternative perspective. This should be presented as a suggestion rather than a directive, encouraging the teenager to consider other possibilities without feeling pressured. The goal is to guide them toward a more balanced approach that could benefit them in the long run.

Example: "I found taking breaks and trying new activities also helped me feel refreshed. Would you be open to exploring some new interests together?"

Why the Feel-Felt-Found Strategy Works

The effectiveness of the Feel-Felt-Found strategy lies in its empathetic approach. Teenagers often resist advice or suggestions because they feel misunderstood or dismissed. This strategy counters resistance by first validating their emotions, which is a critical step in effective communication. Teenagers who feel heard are more likely to be receptive to new ideas.

Moreover, sharing a personal experience humanizes the interaction. Teenagers often view adults as out of touch with their current experiences. By relating to them on a personal level, you break down this barrier and establish common ground.

Finally, by offering a solution as a suggestion rather than a command, you empower the teenager to make their own decisions. This approach respects their growing autonomy while gently guiding them toward healthier choices.

Applying the Strategy in Real-Life Scenarios

The Feel-Felt-Found strategy can be applied in various situations, from everyday challenges to more significant behavioral issues. Here's an example of how this strategy can be used in a real-life scenario.

Scenario: A teenager spends excessive time on gaming, leading to neglect of schoolwork and other responsibilities.

Conversation:

You: "I understand gaming helps you relax after a long day. It's your way of unwinding, and that's important."

Teenager: "Yeah, it's what I enjoy, and it helps me forget about school stress."

You: "I felt the same way about my hobbies when I was your age. I loved spending hours on them because they made me forget everything else."

Teenager: "Exactly! It's my escape."

You: "I found that taking breaks and trying new activities, even just for a little while, helped me feel even more refreshed. It didn't take away from what I enjoyed; it added to it. Would you be open to trying something new together to see if it works for you, too?"

Teenager: "I don't know . . . maybe. What do you have in mind?"

This conversation reveals how the Feel-Felt-Found strategy can create a dialogue rather than a lecture, encouraging teenagers to explore new perspectives while feeling supported and understood.

2. The If . . . Then . . . Strategy

The If . . . Then . . . communication strategy is a powerful tool for parents and educators aiming to guide teenagers through the complexities of decision-making. By linking actions with consequences, this approach helps teenagers understand the impact of their choices and encourages them to think critically about their behavior. The strategy's emphasis on collaboration and problem-solving fosters a positive and respectful relationship between adults and teenagers.

As teenagers navigate the challenges of growing up, the If . . . Then . . . strategy can be a reliable framework for guiding them toward responsible and mature decision-making. By setting clear expectations and involving teenagers in the process, you help them make better choices and empower them to take ownership of their actions, laying the foundation for a successful transition into adulthood.

Understanding the If . . . Then . . . Strategy

The If . . . Then . . . strategy is a straightforward communication technique that clearly outlines the potential outcomes of a teenager's actions. It connects a specific behavior (the "If" part) with a logical consequence (the "Then" part), helping the teenager understand the direct impact of their choices. This approach is particularly effective when a teenager's behavior needs adjustment or setting boundaries is necessary.

1. If: The first part of the strategy introduces the behavior or action in question. It sets the stage by identifying the choice or decision that the teenager might make. This step is critical because it frames the conversation around the teenager's actions, making them aware of the cause-and-effect relationship.

Example: "If you continue to game until late . . ."

2. Then: The second part of the strategy outlines the consequence of the behavior. This consequence should be logical, relevant, and directly related to the behavior. The goal is to help the teenager see the natural outcome of their actions and encourage them to consider the long-term effects of their choices.

Example: ". . . you'll probably feel too tired for school the next day."

3. Engagement: While not explicitly part of the If . . . Then . . . structure, engaging the teenager in a discussion about potential solutions or alternatives is essential. This step invites the teenager to participate in problem-solving, which nurtures a sense of ownership and responsibility for their decisions.

Example: "What do you think we can do to avoid that?"

Why the If . . . Then . . . Strategy Works

The If . . . Then . . . strategy is effective because it provides clarity and structure in communication. Teenagers are often in a phase of life where they are testing boundaries and seeking independence. However, they may not always fully understand the consequences of their actions. By using this strategy, you can help them see the logical outcomes of their choices in a neither punitive nor judgmental way.

One key strength of the If . . . Then . . . approach is that it avoids confrontation. Instead of dictating what the teenager should or should not do, it presents the situation as a choice, allowing the teenager to decide how to proceed. This method respects their growing autonomy while still guiding them toward responsible behavior.

Additionally, involving the teenager in finding solutions creates an opportunity for collaborative problem-solving. This strengthens the parent-child relationship and teaches valuable skills in negotiation and compromise.

Applying the Strategy in Real-Life Scenarios

The If . . . Then . . . strategy can be applied in various scenarios, from everyday habits to more significant decisions. Here's an example of how this strategy can be effectively used:

Scenario: A teenager spends excessive time gaming late into the night, which results in fatigue and poor school performance.

Conversation:

You: "If you continue to game until late, you'll probably feel too tired for school the next day. What do you think we can do to avoid that?"

Teenager: "A timer will mess up my game. I must complete a level before stopping to save my progress."

You: "I get that stopping mid-game isn't ideal. How about we set a gaming schedule that ends before it gets too late so you can finish your sessions and still get enough sleep?"

Teenager: "I guess we could try that. Maybe I can set an alarm to remind me to stop."

This conversation demonstrates how the If . . . Then . . . strategy can guide a teenager toward making better choices without making them feel like they are being forced into compliance. The teenager is made aware of the potential consequences of their actions and invited to contribute to finding a solution that works for both parties.

3. The What If Strategy

The What If communication strategy is a versatile and effective tool for guiding teenagers through the complexities of decision-making. This approach promotes critical thinking, autonomy, and self-reflection by encouraging them to explore alternative scenarios and their potential outcomes.

In a world where teenagers are often faced with challenging choices and external pressures, the What If strategy empowers them to make informed decisions. By supporting them in this exploratory process, you help them develop the skills they need to navigate their lives with confidence and resilience.

The What If strategy provides a framework for respectful and meaningful dialogue as teenagers continue to grow and seek their paths. It helps them consider the impact of their choices and fosters a collaborative relationship built on trust, understanding, and mutual respect.

Understanding the What If Strategy

The What If strategy is a communication method that poses hypothetical scenarios to encourage teenagers to consider the consequences of different actions or decisions. Instead of directly telling them what to do, you guide them to explore various possibilities and their outcomes. This approach shifts the conversation from a directive to an exploratory dialogue, allowing teenagers to feel more in control of their decisions while still being supported by a guiding hand.

1. Introducing the Scenario: The first step in the What If strategy is to present a hypothetical situation that encourages the teenager to consider a different course of action. This scenario should be

relevant to their current behavior or decisions, making it easy for them to engage with the idea.

Example: "What if you tried reducing your gaming time for a week and saw how it affects your mood and energy levels?"

2. Encouraging Exploration: After presenting the scenario, the next step is to encourage the teenager to think through the potential outcomes. This is where you can discuss the possible benefits or challenges that they might encounter, helping them weigh the pros and cons of the proposed scenario.

Example: "We could track the changes together."

3. Offering Support: It's important to acknowledge that trying something new or considering a change can be challenging for teenagers. You can offer your support, and they can rely on you for guidance and encouragement.

Example: "Change can be challenging, but I'll support you through it. Let's start small and make adjustments based on how you feel."

Why the What If Strategy Works

The What If strategy works by tapping into a teenager's natural curiosity and desire for autonomy. By framing the conversation around hypothetical scenarios, you shift the focus from what they should do to what they could do, opening the door for them to consider alternatives on their terms.

This strategy also promotes critical thinking. Teenagers are often in a stage of life where they are learning to navigate complex social and personal decisions. By encouraging them to explore different outcomes, the What If strategy helps them develop the ability to think ahead, anticipate consequences, and make more thoughtful decisions.

Moreover, the What If approach respects the teenager's growing independence. Instead of imposing a solution, you invite them to participate in problem-solving. This makes them more likely to consider your suggestions and strengthens their decision-making skills.

Applying the Strategy in Real-Life Scenarios

The What If strategy can be applied in various scenarios, from everyday decisions to more significant life choices. Here's an example of how this strategy can be used effectively:

Scenario: A teenager spends too much time gaming, affecting their sleep and school performance.

Conversation:

You: "What if you tried reducing your gaming time for a week and saw how it affects your mood and energy levels? We could track the changes together."

Teenager: "I could try that, but it might be hard."

You: "Change can be challenging, but I'll support you through it. Let's start small and make adjustments based on how you feel. We can review how it's going at the end of the week and decide what to do next."

Teenager: "Okay, I'll give it a shot."

In this conversation, the What If strategy allows the teenager to consider a new approach without feeling forced or judged. By framing the scenario as an experiment, you clarify that the outcome isn't predetermined and that adjustments can be made based on their experience.

4. The Simple Swap Strategy

The Simple Swap communication strategy is a practical and respectful way to guide teenagers toward healthier and more balanced lifestyles. This approach reduces resistance and encourages positive changes by offering alternatives that complement rather than replace their current activities.

In a world where teenagers are often drawn to habits that may not always serve their long-term well-being, the Simple Swap strategy provides a gentle and effective way to promote better choices. Focusing on balance and collaboration helps teenagers develop healthier routines and strengthens their ability to make thoughtful decisions about how they spend their time.

Understanding the Simple Swap Strategy

The Simple Swap strategy suggests alternative activities that are healthier or more productive than a teenager might typically choose. The goal is to introduce these alternatives in a way that feels like an enhancement rather than a loss. This method acknowledges teenagers' current preferences while guiding them toward better choices.

1. Identifying the Activity: The first step is to recognize the activity or habit that could be improved. This is done without judgment, simply acknowledging what the teenager currently enjoys.

Example: "Instead of gaming all afternoon . . ."

2. Suggesting an Alternative: Next, propose a healthier or more productive alternative to the current activity. This alternative should be appealing and related to the teenager's interests, making it easier for them to accept the change.

Example: ". . . how about we go outside and throw the ball around or go to the rock-climbing gym? It could be fun."

3. Addressing Concerns: Teenagers may have concerns about missing out on what they enjoy, such as socializing with friends. It is important to acknowledge these concerns and offer a solution that balances the current activity and the suggested alternative.

Example: "I understand that your friends are online. We can find a time that works for gaming with friends and enjoying outdoor activities. Balance is key."

Why the Simple Swap Strategy Works

The Simple Swap strategy is effective because it focuses on balance rather than restriction. Teenagers often resist change, especially when something is being taken away. Offering a swap instead of a stop reduces the likelihood of pushback and makes the idea of change more palatable.

This strategy also promotes a healthier lifestyle by introducing alternatives that are beneficial both physically and mentally. For instance, suggesting outdoor activities as an alternative to prolonged screen time encourages physical exercise and provides a mental break from digital engagement.

Additionally, the Simple Swap strategy fosters collaboration. By involving teenagers in the decision-making process and considering their preferences, you show respect for their autonomy. This collaborative approach strengthens the relationship between adults and teenagers, making it more likely that they will be open to future suggestions.

Applying the Strategy in Real-Life Scenarios

The Simple Swap strategy can be applied in various situations where teenagers might benefit from healthier or more balanced habits. Here's an example of how this strategy can be used effectively:

Scenario: A teenager spends most of their free time gaming or watching videos on social media, leading to limited physical activity and reduced outdoor time.

Conversation:

You: "Instead of being on your device all afternoon, how about we go outside and throw the ball around or go to the rock climbing gym? It could be fun."

Teenager: "I guess we could try that, but my friends are online."

You: "I understand that. We can find a time that works for gaming with friends and enjoying outdoor activities. Balance is key. How about we schedule gaming with your friends in the evening and use the afternoon for something active?"

Teenager: "Yeah, that could work. I wouldn't mind getting outside for a bit."

In this conversation, the Simple Swap strategy introduces a new activity without dismissing the teenager's current interests. By suggesting a manageable adjustment rather than a complete overhaul, the teenager is more likely to accept the alternative and incorporate it into their routine.

As teenagers continue to grow and navigate the complexities of adolescence, the Simple Swap strategy offers a valuable tool for parents, educators, and mentors. It empowers young people to find joy and fulfillment in various activities, helping them build a well-rounded and satisfying life.

5. The How Will We Know? Strategy

The How Will We Know? communication strategy is a powerful tool for fostering collaboration and responsibility in teenagers. This approach encourages critical thinking and mutual respect by involving them in defining and evaluating solutions.

In a world where teenagers increasingly seek independence, the How Will We Know? strategy offers a way to guide them without imposing rigid rules. By creating a transparent and fair process for evaluating outcomes, this method helps teenagers develop the skills they need to make informed decisions and adjust their behavior as necessary.

As teenagers navigate the challenges of growing up, the How Will We Know? strategy provides a framework for constructive and supportive communication. It helps them understand the impact of their choices and strengthens their ability to work collaboratively toward positive outcomes, both in their family life and beyond.

Understanding the How We Know? Strategy

The How Will We Know? strategy is designed to assess the success of a solution in a clear, measurable way. It involves asking the teenager how both parties will know if a plan or decision is working. This approach encourages the teenager to think ahead and consider the outcomes of their choices while providing a structured way to revisit and adjust the plan if needed.

1. Establishing Agreement: The first step is establishing common ground by identifying the issue and agreeing on its impact. This ensures that both the parent and teenager understand the problem and are on the same page about the need for a solution.

Example: "We agree that gaming before bed makes you tired in the morning."

2. Proposing a Solution: Next, involve the teenager in proposing a solution. This step is crucial because it gives them a sense of ownership over the decision, making them more likely to follow through with the plan.

Example: "What do you think would be a solution?" (You would like your child to stop gaming by 8 p.m.).

3. Defining Success: Once a solution is proposed, ask the teenager how they will know if the plan is working. This question encourages them to think critically about the outcomes and establish clear success criteria.

Example: "How will we know if that plan works?"

4. Monitoring and Adjustment: Finally, agree on a trial period to test the solution and discuss the possibility of adjustments if the plan doesn't work as expected. This step ensures the solution is flexible and can be refined based on actual results.

Example: "Okay, let's try that for a week and see how it goes. Would you try stopping at 8 p.m. if it's not working?"

Why the How Will We Know? Strategy Works

The How Will We Know? strategy effectively transforms potential conflicts into collaborative problem-solving opportunities. Teenagers often resist directives that feel imposed upon them, but when involved in creating and evaluating a plan, they are more likely to take responsibility for the outcome.

This strategy also promotes critical thinking by asking teenagers to consider how they will measure success. Instead of simply complying with a rule, they are encouraged to reflect on the practical implications of their choices. This reflection helps them understand the consequences of their actions and prepares them for independent decision-making in the future.

Furthermore, the How Will We Know? approach advances a sense of fairness. By agreeing to evaluate the plan together, parents and teenagers understand that the solution is not set in stone and can be adjusted if it doesn't work. This flexibility reduces the likelihood of conflict and strengthens the parent-child relationship.

Applying the Strategy in Real-Life Scenarios

The How Will We Know? strategy can be applied when a teenager's behavior needs adjustment or a new routine is introduced. Here's an example of how this strategy can be used effectively:

Scenario: A teenager is staying up late gaming, which affects their ability to wake up on time for school.

Conversation:

You: "We agree that gaming before bed makes you tired in the morning. What do you think would be a solution?" (You would like your child to stop gaming by 8 p.m.).

Teenager: "I'll stop gaming by 9 p.m."

You: "How will we know if that plan works?"

Teenager: "If I can get up without your help and be ready to leave for school on time."

You: "Okay, let's try that for a week and see how it goes. Would you try stopping at 8 p.m. if it's not working?"

Teenager: "That sounds fair."

In this conversation, the How Will We Know? strategy transforms what could have been a directive into a collaborative effort. By defining success together, the teenager is more likely to take ownership of the solution and be open to adjustments if needed.

Chapter Eight

Practical Boundary Setting for Healthy Online Habits

In today's digitally driven world, setting boundaries around online habits is crucial for ensuring children develop healthy, balanced relationships with technology. However, the success of these boundaries largely depends on how they are communicated and enforced. Engaging in open, collaborative conversations with your child about these boundaries and the associated expectations is critical to achieving understanding, cooperation, and long-term success.

The Importance of Open Dialogue

When establishing boundaries for online habits, the dialogue between parent and child must remain open and collaborative. An authoritarian approach that imposes rules without input can lead to resistance, while an overly lenient stance may result in a lack of structure. The goal is to find a middle ground where the child feels heard and involved in decision-making, making them more likely to adhere to the agreed-upon guidelines.

Using Negotiation Strategies

Negotiation is a vital tool in these discussions. Using the strategies in Chapters 4, 5, 6, and 7, you will approach the conversation as a partnership rather than a directive. Encourage your child to take ownership of their online habits. This approach advances a sense of responsibility and builds trust and mutual respect, which is essential for practical boundary setting.

Here's an example of how to conduct such a conversation:

You: "Based on our agreement, waking up on time for school was a part of our plan. Today, I noticed you struggled with this. Let's think about what adjustments we might need to make to your gaming schedule to help you meet this goal."

In this scenario, the parent acknowledges the issue without placing blame and invites the child to find a solution. This approach shifts the focus from punishment to problem-solving, making the child a partner in the process.

Encouraging Collaboration and Ownership

It is crucial to make your child a partner in the boundary-setting process. When children feel they have a say in the rules that affect them, they are more likely to follow those rules. This sense of ownership can be nurtured by involving them in every step of the process—from setting the boundaries to determining the consequences of not adhering to them.

For example, you might say:

You: "We both agree that getting enough sleep is important. Since staying up late to game has affected your mornings, what would be a fair adjustment to your gaming schedule?"

By framing the conversation this way, you give your child a stake in the outcome, which can lead to more thoughtful and deliberate decision-making on their part.

Setting Clear Boundaries and Expectations

While collaboration is important, it's also crucial to establish clear, nonnegotiable boundaries. Children should understand that certain expectations must be met, such as maintaining academic performance or fulfilling household responsibilities. However, these boundaries should be presented as part of a broader agreement rather than rigid rules imposed without input.

To achieve this, clearly communicate the expectations and ensure your child understands why they are in place. For example:

You: "I know gaming is something you enjoy, and I want you to have time for it. At the same time, your schoolwork and getting enough sleep are important. Let's work together to figure out a schedule that allows you to do both."

This approach reinforces the idea that boundaries are not arbitrary but are designed to support your child's overall well-being.

Discussing Consequences

Consequences are a natural part of any boundary-setting process, and discussing these openly with your child is essential. As with the boundaries, the conversation about consequences should be collaborative. Please make sure your child understands that consequences are not about punishment but are meant to guide them toward healthier habits.

For instance:

You: "We agreed that if staying up late to game makes it hard for you to wake up for school, we would need to reduce your gaming time. What do you think would be a fair amount of time to cut back?"

By involving your child in this decision, you help them see the connection between their actions and the consequences, making it more likely that they will respect the boundaries set.

Building Trust and Mutual Respect

The foundation of any successful boundary-setting process is trust and mutual respect. When children feel that their opinions are valued and that their parents are working with them rather than against them, they are more likely to engage positively with the process. This trust is built through consistent, respectful communication and honoring the agreements made during these discussions.

For example:

You: "I appreciate that you've been trying to stick to the gaming schedule we agreed on. Let's keep working on this together and make adjustments as needed."

Acknowledging your child's efforts reinforces positive behavior and shows you recognize their commitment to the process.

Components of a Successful Boundary Plan

1. Regular Check-ins

Regular check-ins are an invaluable tool in the ongoing effort to manage teenagers' screen time effectively. Parents can create a structured yet flexible approach that encourages open communication and continuous improvement by incorporating the "How will we know?" strategy and setting clear performance metrics. These weekly or biweekly sessions provide a vital touch-point for reflection, guidance, and support, helping teenagers develop healthier habits and a more balanced lifestyle.

The Role of Regular Check-Ins

Regular check-ins are a structured forum for discussing the teenager's progress and challenges regarding screen time limits. Unlike daily quick check-ins that might focus on immediate issues, these sessions are designed to be more in-depth and occur weekly or biweekly. They provide an opportunity to review the past week, discuss any difficulties encountered, and reinforce positive behaviors.

Establishing a consistent schedule for these check-ins, similar to a performance review in a professional setting, sets clear expectations. This helps hold the teenager accountable and signals the importance of the issue at hand.

Incorporating the "How Will We Know?" Strategy

One of the critical elements of successful check-ins is the "How will we know?" strategy. This approach emphasizes setting measurable performance metrics, which can be used to gauge the teenager's progress. These metrics could include the number of hours spent on screens, completion of schoolwork, participation in physical activities, or even sleep quality. By agreeing on these metrics beforehand, the parent and the teenager can objectively assess whether the boundaries are respected and adjustments are needed.

Setting Performance Metrics

To make the check-ins effective, it is important to establish clear, achievable performance metrics. Here are some examples:

Screen Time: Track the number of hours spent on screens each day, with the goal of gradually reducing this.

Academic Performance: Monitor assignment completion and participation in class activities, ensuring screen time does not interfere with school responsibilities.

Chores and Responsibilities: Assess the teenager's participation in household chores, ensuring that screen time does not take precedence over these duties.

Physical and Social Activities: Track involvement in physical exercise, hobbies, or social interactions, which are critical to a balanced lifestyle.

These metrics should be specific, measurable, and agreed upon by both parties. By doing so, the teenager can understand what is expected and recognize their progress or areas needing improvement.

Structuring the Check-In Conversation

During the check-in, parents should ask a series of reflective questions that encourage open communication. These might include:

1. How did this week go? – This broad question invites the teenager to share their overall experience, providing insight into their general mood and mindset.

2. What challenges did you face? – This question encourages children to identify specific obstacles they encountered, whether related to screen time, school, or personal life.

3. What did you enjoy about this week? – Highlighting positive experiences helps reinforce good habits and shows the teenager that the check-in is not solely focused on criticism.

4. How was your gaming (or other screen activities) this week? – This question targets the central issue of screen time, allowing children to reflect on their behavior and its impact.

5. How do you feel about your chores and schoolwork? – Addressing responsibilities directly ensures that these areas are not neglected in favor of screen time.

Reflect and Respond

After the teenager shares their thoughts, reflecting on what they have said without judgment is essential. Understanding their perspective is critical to maintaining a constructive dialogue. Once they have had the opportunity to express themselves, parents can share their observations, focusing on the positives and areas needing improvement. The tone should remain supportive and encouraging, guiding the teenager toward making better choices rather than simply enforcing rules.

Guiding the Conversation Toward Improvement

The final part of the check-in should involve setting goals for the coming week. Based on the discussion, parents and teenagers can collaboratively identify areas to work on, whether reducing screen time, improving focus on schoolwork, or engaging in more physical activities. By setting these goals together, teenagers are more likely to feel invested in the process and motivated to succeed.

2. Rewards

Incorporating rewards into a boundary plan for reducing screen time can be a highly effective strategy. By setting clear goals and offering meaningful, non-digital rewards, parents can motivate their children to adhere to screen time limits while promoting positive behaviors in other areas of their lives. The key to success lies in thoughtful planning, clear communication, and ongoing collaboration with your child, ensuring that the rewards system supports the ultimate goal of healthier screen time habits.

The Role of Rewards in a Boundary Plan

Rewards are powerful tools for reinforcing positive behaviors, such as adhering to screen time limits. When used appropriately, they can serve as incentives encouraging children to meet the goals set within a boundary plan. Rewards motivate children to follow the rules and create a sense of accomplishment and pride when they achieve their goals.

However, the key to successfully using rewards lies in their thoughtful selection and implementation. It is important to choose rewards that are meaningful to the child but do not inadvertently reinforce the behavior you're trying to limit, such as excessive gaming.

Setting Clear Rewards for Meeting Goals

The first step in incorporating rewards into a boundary plan is to set clear and achievable goals. These goals should be specific, measurable, and agreed upon by both the parent and the child. Once the goals are established, the next step is to decide on appropriate rewards for meeting these goals.

When choosing rewards, selecting options supporting the overall objective of reducing screen time is crucial. For example, consider alternatives that promote healthy, offline activities instead of offering additional gaming time or a new video game as a reward. Some examples include:

Special Outings: Plan a day trip to a place your child enjoys, such as a zoo, mini-golf, go carts, museum, or amusement park.

New Books: Encourage a love of reading by rewarding your child with a book of their choice.

Hobby Supplies: Support your child's interests in non-digital hobbies by providing supplies or tools, such as art materials or sports equipment.

Example Conversation for Discussing Rewards

Introducing the concept of rewards into your boundary plan should be a collaborative process. Engaging your child in the discussion ensures they feel invested in the goals and the rewards. Here's an example of how such a conversation might go:

You: "If our check-ins continue to go well for the next month, what are you hoping to work toward as a reward?"

Child: "I'd really like a new computer."

You: "That's a big reward. Let's talk about what we expect in terms of your grades and participation at home to consider that."

This conversation sets the stage for goal-setting and opens up a dialogue about the level of effort required to earn a significant reward. It's important to balance the reward with the difficulty of the goals, ensuring that your child understands the value of their hard work.

Establishing Expectations and Criteria

When discussing rewards, you must set clear expectations and criteria that your child must meet to earn the reward. This includes specific performance metrics, such as:

Screen Time Adherence: Tracking and staying within the agreed-upon screen time limits.

Academic Performance: Maintaining or improving grades as a reflection of responsible screen time use.

Household Participation: Completing chores and responsibilities without reminders or delays.

By establishing these criteria, you create a structured framework that helps your child understand what is required to earn the reward. It also reinforces that rewards are not simply for following the rules but for exceeding expectations and demonstrating responsible behavior.

Monitoring Progress and Adjusting Rewards

As with any boundary plan, monitoring progress is crucial. Regular check-ins allow you to assess how well your child adheres to the screen time limits and other criteria. During these check-ins, you can discuss any challenges they've faced, celebrate successes, and adjust goals or rewards as necessary.

If your child consistently meets or exceeds expectations, you might consider increasing the reward or setting a new, more challenging goal. Conversely, if your child is struggling, you might need to adjust the goals to make them more attainable or offer smaller, more frequent rewards to maintain motivation.

3. Negative Consequences

Negative consequences are necessary for a successful boundary plan for managing a child's screen time. When implemented thoughtfully and consistently, they serve as effective guardrails that keep children on track and help them develop healthier habits. By clearly defining and discussing these consequences with your child, you create a framework that encourages responsibility, balance, and long-term success in managing screen time.

The Role of Negative Consequences in a Boundary Plan

Negative consequences help reinforce the importance of adhering to agreed-upon rules and demonstrate that actions have consequences. When children understand that failing to meet their responsibilities leads to specific, predetermined outcomes, they are more likely to take the rules seriously and strive to stay within the set boundaries.

However, it is essential to approach negative consequences with the right mindset. These measures should not be seen as punishments but as natural outcomes encouraging children to make better choices. The goal is not to create a sense of fear or resentment but to help children understand the importance of balance and responsibility in using screen time.

Examples of Negative Consequences

When establishing a boundary plan, defining clear and logical consequences for not respecting the agreed-upon limits is crucial. Here are some examples of negative consequences that can be effectively implemented:

1. Decreased Gaming Time: If a child exceeds their screen time limits or fails to complete their responsibilities, reducing their allowed gaming time can be a natural consequence. This measure helps reinforce the idea that screen time is a privilege that must be earned.

2. Restrictions on Specific Devices or Platforms: Limiting access to certain devices or platforms that are particularly problematic can be an effective way to address overuse. For example, restricting access to those apps can help redirect their focus to more productive activities if social media is consuming too much of your child's time.

3. Additional Chores: Assigning extra chores as a consequence can help instill a sense of responsibility. This approach serves as a deterrent and encourages children to contribute more actively to household tasks.

4. Restrictions on Social Activities: Limiting participation in social activities, such as sleepovers or outings with friends, can be a powerful consequence of not adhering to screen time rules. This measure underscores the importance of meeting responsibilities before enjoying leisure activities.

5. Limited Phone Access or Downgrading to a Basic Phone: In cases where screen time boundaries are repeatedly violated, limiting phone access or downgrading to a basic phone can be an effective consequence. This action directly addresses the issue and serves as a strong reminder of the importance of responsible device use.

Discussing Consequences with Your Child

I think it's important to talk about these potential consequences with your child before they are implemented. This conversation should be clear, direct, and free of anger or frustration. The goal is to ensure that your child understands that these consequences are a natural result of not meeting their responsibilities, not arbitrary punishments.

Here's how a conversation about negative consequences might unfold:

You: "We've set clear boundaries around screen time and must stick to them. If these boundaries aren't respected, there will be consequences, like less gaming time or restrictions on your phone. These aren't meant to punish you, but to help you stay on track with your responsibilities."

Child: "But I don't want to lose my gaming time."

You: "I understand, and that's why it's important to follow the rules we've set together. These consequences will only come into play if the boundaries aren't respected. Our goal is to help you develop good habits, and staying within these limits is part of that."

By having this conversation, you set clear expectations and ensure your child understands the link between their behavior and the consequences. This clarity helps prevent misunderstandings and reduces the likelihood of conflict when a consequence needs to be enforced.

Implementing and Enforcing Consequences

Once consequences are established, it's important to enforce them consistently. Inconsistency can undermine the boundary plan, leading to confusion and diminishing the effectiveness of the consequences. When a boundary is violated, calmly and firmly apply the agreed-upon consequence without negotiation or hesitation. This consistency reinforces the seriousness of the rules and helps your child understand that these boundaries are nonnegotiable.

Encouraging Better Habits Through Consequences

The ultimate goal of implementing negative consequences is to encourage better habits and more responsible behavior. Over time, as your child adjusts to the boundaries and the associated consequences, they should develop a greater sense of self-regulation. This process may take time and patience, but it is critical to helping your child develop a balanced approach to screen time and other responsibilities.

Conducting conversations about boundaries and expectations is a critical component of setting up healthy online habits for children. You create a framework that encourages responsibility, trust, and mutual respect by maintaining an open and collaborative dialogue, using negotiation strategies, and involving your child in the decision-making process. These conversations help establish clear boundaries and empower your child to take ownership of their online behavior, leading to healthier and more balanced habits in the long run.

Setting Limits for Younger Kids

Parents must establish boundaries and controls as children explore the digital world through online video games to ensure a safe and balanced experience. Younger kids, in particular, need guidance to navigate these platforms responsibly, and there are several proactive steps parents can take to prevent potential issues. Setting clear screen time limits and controlling the gaming environment can help your child develop healthy digital habits while safeguarding them from inappropriate content and interactions.

Limiting or Disabling Voice-Chat Features

One of the most significant risks for younger kids playing online video games is exposure to inappropriate conversations or harmful interactions through voice chat. Many games offer voice chat features that allow players to communicate with each other in real-time. While this can enhance the gaming experience, it also opens the door to potentially harmful exchanges with strangers.

To protect your child, consider limiting or completely turning off voice-chat features on your home gaming system. Most video games have "sound settings" where you can entirely turn off voice chat. Some games allow you to mute individual players, but turning off voice chat completely is often the best approach for younger kids. This prevents them from talking to anyone they don't know, reducing the risk of exposure to inappropriate language or behavior.

Enforcing the Use of Speakers Instead of Headphones

Another effective strategy for managing your child's screen time and online behavior is to require them to use speakers instead of headphones while gaming. This allows you to hear what's happening in the game whenever you walk by, giving you a better understanding of the content and interactions your child is experiencing.

Kids who use headphones may feel more isolated and less accountable for their actions, as no one else can hear what's happening. By enforcing the use of speakers, you create an environment where they are less likely to engage in inappropriate activities, knowing that others in the household can hear what's happening.

Monitoring the Gaming Environment

In addition to hearing what's happening during gameplay, it's equally important to visually monitor the gaming environment. Where your child plays video games can significantly impact their behavior and the amount of time they spend gaming. Studies have shown that having a game system in a child's bedroom can increase usage by up to fifty percent, making it harder to control screen time and monitor their behavior.

To maintain better control over your child's gaming habits, keep the gaming area in a shared space where you can easily see what's on the screen. This might be the living room or another shared area in the home. By keeping the gaming console visible, you can quickly step in if something inappropriate appears on the screen or your child is playing longer than agreed.

If your child already has a game console in their bedroom, especially if they play with the door closed, it's important to reconsider this setup. Moving the console to a more visible area of the house can significantly reduce the time they spend gaming and improve your ability to monitor their activities.

Establishing Screen Time Limits

In addition to controlling the gaming environment, setting clear screen time limits is essential for younger kids. These limits should be realistic and based on your child's age, developmental stage, and daily schedule. For younger children, it's often recommended to limit screen time to one hour per day on school days and slightly more on weekends. These limits ensure that gaming does not interfere with other important activities such as homework, physical exercise, and family time.

Be consistent in enforcing these limits and communicate the rules clearly to your child. Let them know why these boundaries are in place and how they help them develop a healthy relationship with technology. Involving your child in setting these rules can also make them more likely to comply, as they'll feel a sense of ownership over their screen time.

Chapter Nine
Understanding Boundary Setting in Parenting

In today's digital world, managing a child's screen time is a significant challenge for many parents. Establishing boundaries is crucial in ensuring children develop healthy habits and maintain a balanced lifestyle. However, despite the best intentions, many boundary plans fail. The primary reason is often simple: the boundaries weren't consistently enforced. This failure not only undermines the original goals, such as reducing video game playtime, but it also sends a message to the child that the rules are flexible and can be bent or ignored.

Why Do Most Boundary Plans Fail?

Understanding the reasons behind the failure of boundary plans is essential for creating a more practical approach. Here are some of the most common pitfalls:

1. Inconsistent Enforcement

One of the most common reasons boundary plans fail is inconsistent enforcement. This can happen for various reasons—parents may lapse in their follow-through, give in to resistance from the child, or relax the rules prematurely because things seem to be improving. When boundaries are not firmly upheld, it teaches children that these rules are negotiable. This inconsistency undermines the specific boundary and erodes the trust and respect in the parent-child relationship. Children learn quickly that if they push hard enough or wait long enough, the rules may change, making it even more challenging to enforce boundaries in the future.

2. Unrealistic Goals

Another common issue is setting unrealistic goals. Sometimes, parents set targets more akin to wish lists rather than achievable objectives. These goals may be too ambitious, such as suddenly expecting a child who spends several hours a day on screens to reduce that time to 30 minutes. When goals are unattainable, it sets both the parent and child up for failure, leading to frustration and a sense of defeat. Setting realistic, incremental goals that can be consistently met and gradually adjusted over time is important.

3. Lack of Enforcement

Failing to enforce the set boundaries consistently is a significant reason for boundary plans collapsing. Without consistent enforcement, children quickly learn that these guidelines are flexible and may not need to be followed. This lack of structure can lead to confusion and resentment, as children may struggle to understand the expectations and the consequences of not meeting them. Consistent enforcement is crucial for maintaining the integrity of the boundary plan and ensuring that it serves its intended purpose.

4. Emotion-Driven Decisions

Setting boundaries in frustration, anger, or desperation often leads to unrealistic expectations and unachievable goals. When emotions run high, parents might set overly strict or punitive boundaries, which can be difficult to enforce and may not address the underlying issues effectively. This approach can lead to a cycle of setting and breaking boundaries, further eroding the effectiveness of the boundary plan and damaging the parent-child relationship.

The 25 Percent Rule for Achievable Goals

Setting boundaries for a child's screen time is essential for creating a healthy balance between digital activities and other aspects of life. However, one of the most common pitfalls in this process is setting overly ambitious, difficult goals to achieve and maintain. The "25 Percent Rule" can be an effective strategy to combat this tendency and create a more sustainable approach. This rule focuses on gradual, manageable changes that lead to long-term success.

The 25 Percent Rule is a simple yet powerful method for setting achievable goals in boundary setting. Rather than aiming for drastic reductions in screen time all at once, this rule advocates for making smaller, incremental changes—specifically, a 25% reduction in the undesired behavior. This approach allows for gradual adjustment, making it easier for the child and the parent to adapt to the new boundaries.

Why the 25 Percent Rule Works

The 25 Percent Rule works because it acknowledges the challenges of making significant lifestyle changes, particularly regarding ingrained habits like screen time. Focusing on small, manageable reductions minimizes resistance and helps build momentum through a series of small victories. As the child begins to see the benefits of these changes—such as more time for other activities, improved focus, or better sleep—they become more open to further adjustments.

Steps to Implement the 25 Percent Rule

Implementing the 25 Percent Rule involves a few straightforward steps, each designed to make reducing screen time more achievable and sustainable.

1. Initial Reduction

The first step in the 25 Percent Rule is to identify the current amount of screen time and then reduce it by 25%. For example, if a child spends four hours playing video games on weekdays, the initial goal would be to reduce this to three hours. This reduction is significant enough to make a difference but not so drastic that it feels unattainable.

By starting with a 25% reduction, you set a realistic and measurable goal. This initial change allows the child to experience the impact of the new boundary without feeling overwhelmed, making it more likely that they will adhere to the plan.

2. Evaluate and Adjust

After implementing the initial reduction, it's important to evaluate its impact. Observe how the child adjusts to the new boundary and discuss their feelings and experiences. This step is crucial for understanding whether the new limit works as intended or needs further adjustments.

You can negotiate further reductions based on this evaluation, again following the 25 Percent Rule. For instance, if the child has successfully adjusted to three hours of gaming, the next step might be to reduce this time by another 25%, bringing it down to 2.25 hours. This gradual approach ensures that each reduction is manageable and allows the child to adapt at a comfortable pace.

3. Repeat the Process

The key to the 25 Percent Rule is repetition. Continue reducing screen time in stages, each time cutting back by 25% of the remaining time. By doing so, you gradually move closer to the ultimate goal, whether reducing gaming time to one hour a day or limiting overall screen time to a certain number of hours per week.

This staged approach makes the overall goal more manageable and achievable. Each step forward builds on the success of the previous one, helping to reinforce the new boundaries and making it easier for the child to accept further reductions.

The Benefits of the 25 Percent Rule

The 25 Percent Rule offers several key benefits that make it an effective strategy for boundary setting:

Manageable Change: The 25 Percent Rule makes change more manageable for both the child and the parent by focusing on small, incremental reductions. This approach reduces the likelihood of resistance and helps maintain a positive attitude toward the new boundaries.

Small Victories: Each 25% reduction represents a small victory, which can boost the child's confidence and motivation. These successes demonstrate that the new boundaries are achievable and beneficial, making further reductions more palatable.

Sustainable Progress: The 25 Percent Rule encourages gradual change, which is more likely to lead to sustainable progress. Rather than imposing drastic limits that may be difficult to maintain, this approach builds a foundation for long-term success.

Flexibility: The 25 Percent Rule allows for flexibility in the boundary-setting process. By evaluating and adjusting the limits at each stage, you can tailor the approach to your child's needs and circumstances, ensuring that the boundaries remain effective over time.

Characteristics of Effective Boundary Setting

To create boundaries that are both effective and sustainable, it's essential to focus on several key characteristics: collaborative planning, setting small and achievable goals, maintaining calm and clear communication, and consistent monitoring. Each of these elements plays a crucial role in ensuring that boundaries are respected and that they lead to positive changes in behavior.

1. Collaborative Planning

One of the most critical aspects of boundary setting is involving your child in the planning process. When children are included in goal-setting and decision-making, they are more likely to buy into the boundaries and take ownership of their behavior. This collaborative approach helps to build trust and mutual respect, making it easier to enforce the rules and encouraging the child to adhere to them.

For example, instead of simply dictating how much screen time is allowed, engage your child in a discussion about their current habits and what a reasonable reduction might look like. Ask for their input on structuring their day to include non-screen activities they enjoy. This not only makes the process more democratic but also increases the likelihood of compliance, as the child feels their voice has been heard and their opinions valued.

2. Small, Achievable Goals

Setting small, achievable goals is another critical component of effective boundary setting. Goals that are too ambitious or unrealistic can lead to frustration and resistance. Instead, focus on making incremental changes that feel like wins for both the parent and the child. These small victories help to build momentum and encourage ongoing compliance with the boundaries.

For instance, if your child spends several hours a day on screens, start with a smaller reduction instead of cutting their time in half immediately. As mentioned above, 25% percent reduction would be a good place to start. Once this goal is consistently met, further reductions can be made. This gradual approach makes the change less daunting and more manageable, increasing the likelihood of long-term success.

3. Calm and Clear Communication

Practical boundary setting requires calm and clear communication. It's important to discuss and establish boundaries during quiet moments when the parent and the child can engage in a conversation without distractions or heightened emotions. This ensures that the boundaries are reasonable, understood, and communicated.

When setting boundaries, explain the reasons behind the rules and the benefits of adhering to them. For example, you might say, "We're setting these limits to help you sleep better and have more time for other activities you enjoy, like playing outside or reading." This approach helps the child understand the purpose of the boundaries and how they contribute to their overall well-being.

Additionally, clarity is key—make sure the boundaries are specific and easy to understand. Instead of saying, "You need to spend less time on your phone," set a clear limit, such as "You can use your phone for up to one hour after school, but then it's time to do homework."

4. Consistent Monitoring

Consistency is the cornerstone of successful boundary setting. Once boundaries are set, they need to be consistently monitored and enforced. This involves regularly checking in on your child's progress, providing feedback, and making adjustments as necessary. Consistent monitoring helps ensure that the boundaries are respected and continue to serve their intended purpose.

For example, if the boundary limits gaming to one hour per day, it's important to follow up each day to ensure this limit is being observed. If the child struggles to adhere to the boundary, discuss their challenges and consider making adjustments to the plan. Perhaps the gaming time could be split into two shorter sessions, or a reward system could be introduced to encourage adherence.

Regular check-ins also provide an opportunity to celebrate successes, reinforce positive behavior, and encourage the child to follow the boundaries. By consistently monitoring and enforcing the rules, parents can help their children develop healthier habits and reduce the likelihood of boundary violations.

5. Avoiding Emotionally Driven Decisions

To set effective boundaries, it's important to approach the process calmly and rationally. Avoid making decisions in moments of frustration or anger, as these emotions can cloud judgment and lead to setting unrealistic or overly harsh boundaries. Instead, reflect on the situation and consider the long-term impact of the boundaries you set.

It can be helpful to discuss the boundary plan with your partner or another trusted adult to gain perspective and ensure that the goals and consequences are reasonable and achievable. This approach helps create a boundary plan that is both fair and effective.

Chapter Ten

The Boundary Plan Blueprint

E stablishing a structured screen time boundary plan can help set clear expectations and advance a cooperative environment where your child can learn responsibility, understand the consequences of their actions, and feel supported in their growth. This section outlines a step-by-step approach to creating an effective screen time boundary plan, ensuring you and your child are aligned on goals, boundaries, and expectations.

Step 1: Start the Conversation

The foundation of any successful boundary plan begins with open communication. This step involves engaging your child in a casual conversation to explore their current feelings and habits regarding screen time.

Engage: Initiate a relaxed, nonconfrontational conversation with your child. The goal is to create an environment where they feel comfortable sharing their thoughts.

Inquire: Use open-ended questions to gain insight into their level of satisfaction with their current lifestyle, including their gaming and social media habits. Questions such as "Are you happy with the direction your life is taking?" and "How do you feel about the amount of time you spend on gaming or social media?" can help uncover underlying issues and set the stage for meaningful dialogue.

Goals: Share your family goals, such as spending more time together without the distraction of screens, increasing physical activity, and encouraging face-to-face interactions with friends. Invite your child to share their goals, creating a mutual understanding and a foundation for collaboration.

Step 2: Explore Options

Once the conversation is underway, it's time to explore different options for setting boundaries and achieving the goals you've discussed.

Collaboration: Encourage your child to participate actively in the decision-making process. This involvement increases their sense of ownership and commitment to the plan.

Options Menu: Present a range of choices concerning goals, levers (such as time limits or device restrictions), metrics for success, and milestones. Allow your child to weigh in on these options, helping to tailor the plan to their needs and preferences.

Validation: Discuss how you will both recognize if the plan is effective. Ask questions like, "How will we know if this plan is working?" This dialogue ensures that both parties clearly understand what success looks like and how it will be measured.

Step 3: Develop a Boundary Plan with Input from Your Child

With a solid foundation of communication and collaboration, you can now move on to developing the actual boundary plan.

Collaborative Boundary Setting: While you, as the parent, will ultimately set the boundaries, it's important to involve your child in deciding the first milestone. For instance, ask them, "What aspects of gaming are important to you? Are there specific times when gaming is more enjoyable because your friends are online?"

Set Conditions: Establish conditions based on your child's preferences and your overall goals. For example, you might say, "Homework must be completed before gaming on school nights." This approach ensures that boundaries are reasonable and aligned with your child's daily routine.

Inflexibility on Agreed Boundaries: Once boundaries are set, be firm in enforcing them. Consistency is key to maintaining the plan's integrity and taking it seriously.

Achievable Targets: Use the 25 Percent Rule to set realistic and attainable goals. For instance, if your child currently spends four hours on screens, begin by reducing this to three hours. Gradual reductions are more manageable and increase the likelihood of long-term success.

Step 4: Finalize the Boundary Plan

After developing the boundary plan, it's time to finalize and prepare for implementation.

Clarification of Goals and Milestones: Ensure that all objectives and checkpoints are clearly defined and agreed upon by both you and your child. Clarity at this stage is crucial for preventing misunderstandings later on.

Monitoring: Discuss the tools and methods you'll use to monitor progress. Apps like Ourpact can help manage screen time and provide transparency for parents and children.

Reinforcement: Double-check that you can consistently support and enforce the agreed-upon rules. Consistency in enforcement is critical to the plan's success.

Buy-in: Confirm that your child is fully on board with the plan and understands the importance of following the established boundaries. Their commitment is essential for the plan to work.

Step 5: Institute the Plan, Start Weekly Check-Ins, and Collect Feedback

With the plan in place, it's time to implement and monitor its effectiveness through regular check-ins and feedback.

Implementation: Begin applying the plan immediately and schedule weekly reviews to assess progress. These check-ins provide an opportunity to celebrate successes, address challenges, and make necessary adjustments.

Feedback: Regularly discuss what is working and what isn't. Your child's feedback is invaluable in refining the plan and ensuring that it continues to meet your mutual goals.

Continuity in Success: If the plan is successful, maintain it. Explain to your child that altering a working formula might lead to setbacks, reinforcing the importance of sticking to the agreed boundaries.

Troubleshoot Failures: If the plan is not working as expected, reflect on any emotional reactions, lack of resources, or unexpected events that may have undermined it. Identify the failure points and strategize improvements for future attempts.

Boundary Plan Worksheet

BOUNDARY PLAN

Area of Concern

| Problem | Possible root cause | Solution |

Possible Obstacles

| Obstacle | Solution |

Check-In Schedule

| Date | Goal | Outcome |

Rewards

| Milestone | Reward |

Consequences

| Condition | Consequence |

Total Safety Solutions • All Rights Reserved 2024 • www.CyberSafetyCop.com

We have created a boundary plan worksheet for you. You can download the form from the resource page on our website (www. cybersafetycop.com/downloads). This form is designed to help parents and children collaboratively set boundaries around screen time. It is intended to open communication between both parties, allowing for structured goal-setting, problem-solving, and check-ins to ensure progress. The manual below will guide you through each section of the form, providing examples and tips to fill it out effectively.

1. Area of Concern

Problem:

In this section, you and your child should clearly define the behavior or issue related to screen time that needs improvement. The goal is to pinpoint a specific problem that screen use may contribute to.

Example:

"Waking up late and tired in the morning, leading to a lack of focus in school."

Possible Root Cause:

Together, discuss why this issue is happening. Explore potential root causes by brainstorming and being open with each other. This will help in finding a suitable solution.

Example:

"Going to bed late because homework isn't finished."

"Playing games or watching videos before homework or study time."

Solution:

In this section, the parent and child should agree on a clear, actionable solution to the identified problem. This solution should be achievable, specific, and aimed at resolving the root cause.

Example Solution:

"Complete all homework assignments before playing games or watching videos."

"Turn off screens one hour before bedtime to promote better sleep habits."

2. Possible Obstacles

Obstacle:

Work together to identify any challenges or obstacles that may arise while trying to implement the solution. Make a list of possible obstacles and prioritize them from the most significant to the least.

Example:

"Not enough time to finish homework due to after-school activities."

"Temptation to use the phone or gaming console even when it's not allowed."

Solution:

Once obstacles are listed, brainstorm practical ways to overcome them. Ensure these solutions are realistic and achievable for your child.

Example:

"Set a daily schedule to complete homework right after coming home."

"Create a reward system for staying on track and avoiding screen time before tasks are done."

3. Check-in Schedule

Date:

Plan regular check-ins to review your child's progress. Set specific dates for these check-ins, either weekly or biweekly, depending on your family's schedule. It's important to stick to these dates to maintain consistency.

Example:

Check-ins could be every Sunday evening to assess the progress over the week.

Outcome:

Leave this section blank until your scheduled check-ins. At each check-in, document whether your child has met the goals and what has contributed to their success or struggles.

4. Rewards

Refer to Chapter 10 (if applicable) for our recommendation for rewards. These should be clearly defined and tied to milestones your child can achieve.

Example:

"If all homework is completed before screen time for five consecutive days, I will take you and two friends to mini-golf."

"If bedtime rules are followed consistently for two weeks, you will get a special movie night."

5. Consequences

Consequences should also be discussed as per Chapter 10. These consequences need to be directly related to screen time and enforceable. Ensure they are proportional to the boundary violation and clearly understood by your child.

Example:

"Lose gaming privileges for 24 hours if screens are not turned off on time."

"Move bedtime 30 minutes earlier if they fail to wake up for school without assistance."

Additional Tips:

- Be sure to involve your child in every step of the process. The more ownership they take, the more likely they are to respect the boundaries.

- Stay firm but flexible. Stick to the plan unless something significant arises that requires an adjustment.

- Review and adjust the plan regularly as necessary to ensure it continues to meet your child's needs and is still effective.

Chapter Eleven

Dealing with Resistance and Enforcing Boundaries

Building a strong alliance with your child and establishing a solid boundary plan is crucial, but resistance is inevitable even with the best preparation. Parents often resort to authority to enforce obedience when faced with pushback—whether it's resistance to new rules or a defensive reaction to boundaries. However, when dealing with gaming or other problematic behaviors, it's more effective to empower your child while maintaining control.

Understanding Resistance and Denial

Resistance to screen time boundaries often stems from underlying negative emotions, which can lead to denial as a defense mechanism. For a child deeply invested in gaming, losing access can feel like a significant loss, similar to how someone with an addiction might fear the loss of their substance. Understanding the root causes of resistance and denial is the first step in effectively addressing these behaviors.

Source of Resistance

Resistance is often a reaction to the discomfort or fear associated with change. For children, particularly those who have formed strong attachments to gaming or other online activities, the idea of reducing screen time can evoke feelings of loss, anxiety, or frustration. This emotional response can lead to denial, where the child refuses to acknowledge that their behavior is problematic or that a change is necessary.

Unaware vs. Aware

Children dealing with screen time issues can generally be categorized into two groups:

- Unaware Child: These children are not yet aware they have a problem. Their resistance stems from ignorance— they genuinely do not see the issue and, therefore, argue against the boundaries out of a lack of understanding.

- Aware Child: These children are aware there is a problem but deny its severity due to the emotional discomfort it causes. Their resistance is a way of protecting themselves from the painful reality of the situation. They may understand the logic behind the boundaries but struggle to accept them emotionally.

Strategies for Managing Resistance

Successfully managing resistance requires tailored strategies depending on whether your child is pre-insight or post-insight. The goal is to reduce the emotional charge behind their resistance and guide them toward recognizing the need for change.

For Unaware Children

For children unaware of the problem, it's essential to gently increase their awareness without making them feel attacked. Open-ended questions are an effective tool in this situation.

- Open-Ended Questions: These questions encourage your child to think critically about their behavior and its impact without feeling cornered. For example:

- "How do you feel after spending several hours gaming?"

- "What do you think would happen if you spent a little less time on screens?"

These questions help your child start to see the issue on their own, which is more powerful than being told there is a problem.

For Aware Children

Emotional validation is key for children who are aware of the problem but resist acknowledging it due to emotional discomfort. Reflective listening techniques can help lower their defenses and open the door to a more honest conversation.

- Reflective Listening: This involves acknowledging your child's feelings without immediately countering them. For example, if your child says, "I don't think I spend too much time gaming," you might respond with:

- "I hear that you enjoy gaming, and it's something you look forward to. It's important to have things we enjoy. Can we talk about how we can make sure you still have time for other important things, too?"

This approach helps break down their denial by showing that you understand their perspective, which makes them more likely to consider yours.

Key Approaches

Certain communication techniques can make a significant difference in how your child responds when managing resistance.

- Open-Ended Questions: Engage your child in a dialogue where they feel heard and understood. This reduces their need to defend themselves and makes them more open to considering other perspectives.

- Reflective Listening: Acknowledge your child's feelings without immediately challenging them. This helps to lower their defenses and opens up space for a more constructive conversation.

- Replace "But" with "And": When responding to your child, avoid using "but," which can invalidate their feelings. Instead, use "and" to acknowledge their emotions while introducing your perspective. For example:

Instead of saying, "I understand what you're saying, BUT here's what I think," try, "I understand that your friends are important to you, and you really enjoy gaming, and as a teenager, it's natural to want to have fun. At the same time, it's important to balance that with your responsibilities as a student. How do we find a balance?"

What to Avoid

While managing resistance, certain actions can inadvertently escalate the situation and should be avoided:

- Don't Counter Their Feelings: Avoid making your view a direct counterpoint to theirs, as this can make your child feel that their feelings are being dismissed or invalidated.

- Don't Invalidate Their Emotions: Acknowledge your child's discomfort about cutting back on gaming. Recognizing their feelings helps to diminish their need to deny the problem and can lead to a more open and honest discussion.

Aim for Understanding

When exploring resistance with your child, your goal should be to learn, not prove something. Kids can sense when you're using a question to make a point, and they won't engage if they feel like it's a setup.

Typically, when people ask questions, they do so because they genuinely don't know the answer. This approach—coming from a place of curiosity and ignorance—is what you should adopt when asking your child questions. You're not the expert here; you're learning. And while being ignorant doesn't mean you're power-less, your child understands that you still hold authority. They realize that educating you on what you don't know can work in their favor, while withholding information won't help them.

- DON'T ask a question unless you're genuinely ready to listen to the answer and try to understand it.

- DO honestly attempt to hear your child's perspective and deepen your understanding of their feelings.

TRY THIS: If your child says being on their phone at night is their time to connect with friends, you can say, "I can see how it must be tough when 7 p.m. comes around, and I tell you to put your phone away. It probably feels like you're being cut off from your friends."

This response might surprise your child—after all, here you are, sympathizing with them and trying to understand their viewpoint. Keep going with this: "I understand that chatting with your friends is important to you. I'm happy for you to do that as soon as your homework is finished."

Let's be real: When we're concerned about our kids, we tend to talk more than we listen. We often ask questions to make a point. But what if we switched our approach to asking questions with the goal of understanding instead?

Schedule regular discussions with your child that don't directly impact how much gaming they're allowed. Sometimes, it's necessary to separate boundary enforcement from conversation. If boundary enforcement and discussion are intertwined, your child might be less willing to talk to you. Using the right language can help you set boundaries while encouraging open dialogue.

- DO separate boundary enforcement from empathetic conversation.

- DON'T bring up gaming restrictions during your regular discussions.

TRY THIS: Use open-ended questions, practice reflective listening, and offer emotional validation to help your child feel understood. Here's how that could look:

- Open-ended question: Ask, "What is it about social media that's so important to you?" They might say, "I really enjoy chatting with my friends. It's a lot of fun, and we stay up late talking."

- Reflective listening: Respond with, "It sounds like connecting with your friends is really important to you. Everyone in your group likes to unwind after school by staying up late chatting."

- Emotional validation: Empathize by saying, "That must be tough. You probably feel like you're being cut off from your friends when I set phone restrictions." You could then suggest, "Let's discuss this tomorrow. If we can figure out a way for you to complete everything you need to do, we can be more flexible about your online time with friends."

Notice that you haven't compromised on the rule that homework needs to be done before phone time, but you've shown that you're listening and that you care about your child's feelings.

The purpose of exploring resistance is to uncover what your child values. Here are some more open-ended questions and statements to help you get started, some of which you might have used when you first started building an alliance with your child:

- "Help me understand why playing video games is so important to you."

- "What bothers you about having a limit on your gaming/ social media time?"

- "What do you enjoy so much about video games/ TikTok?"

- "If I set a limit of two hours of homework before gaming, help me understand what feels unfair about that."

Their answers will help you grasp the importance of gaming and social media in their lives and give you insight into their perspective, which you can then incorporate into future boundary-setting conversations.

Changing the dynamic between you and your child regarding gaming involves healthily handling resistance. Sometimes, when faced with a lot of resistance, interactions can spiral into power struggles. You restrict, they react. It becomes an escalating battle where you create stricter rules, and they find ways around them. This is a losing game for everyone involved.

If you use a "my way or the highway" approach, your child will likely adopt the same mindset. You think, "I'm the parent, so I'll do what I want," and they'll respond in kind. This isn't just about asserting control; it's about power dynamics. Your child has become very skilled at this game—because, knowingly or not, it's the game you've been teaching them. Even if you "win," everyone loses.

Instead, see resistance as an opportunity to model the correct behavior to your child. By rolling with their resistance, you can demonstrate a healthier way of handling conflicts and power struggles.

Chapter Twelve

Helping Your Teen Take Responsibility
Failure is an Option

As parents, we're hardwired to be problem solvers. When our child hits a roadblock, our instinct is to step in and fix things, ensuring they avoid failure and disappointment. But here's the thing: this well-intentioned behavior might be doing more harm than good. If we want our children to grow into independent, self-reliant adults, we need to start letting them solve their own problems—even if that means letting them fail sometimes.

Letting Your Child Take the Lead

The idea here is simple but powerful: instead of solving your child's problems for them, encourage them to figure out their own solutions. Yes, it can be challenging to step back, especially when you've always been the one to sign them up for activities, drive them to lessons, and make sure everything runs smoothly. But as your child grows older, their need for independence increases, and so does your responsibility to let them navigate their challenges on their own.

Understanding the Gaming Equation: Fun + Problems

For most people, gaming starts as a fun way to unwind and enjoy themselves. The "equation" looks like this:

Gaming = Fun

But when gaming begins to interfere with responsibilities, it transforms into:

Gaming = Fun + Problems

These problems can range from minor, like missing a school assignment, to major, like flunking out of college. When the problems outweigh the fun, people start to make a change. The old saying, "Change doesn't start until you hit rock bottom," is true.

As parents, our instinct is to shield our children from these problems. We swoop in, fix the issue, and remove the "problems" from the equation, leaving our child with just the fun part:

Gaming = Fun

But here's the catch: this cycle can't continue forever. In fact, the longer you delay your child from realizing the cost of their behaviors, the worse it will get, and the harder their fall will be. I've seen this play out many times in families when they have a child who is dealing with addiction. Their child loses their job and their apartment because of their addiction. The parents let them live at home. The parents bail them out of jail and pay their court fees. Sooner or later, your child must face the consequences of their actions. The earlier they learn this lesson, the better. Don't wait until they're in their thirties to let them face failure. The goal is to help them become independent and capable of regulating their behavior—whether it's gaming, social media, drugs, or other areas of their life.

Real-Life Example: Reinforcing the Wrong Behaviors

My goal is to help your child become independent and regulate their gaming/social media behavior. A big part of engendering their independence is letting them come up with their own solutions.

We, as parents, could be better at this. Frequently, if kids do poorly in school, the parents will jump in to take on the responsibility of helping them achieve success. Here is an example my friend shared with me. His son told him he had a project due the following day, even though it had been assigned two weeks earlier. The assignment was to create a main course dish from scratch that represented his heritage and bring it to school to share in a classroom potluck. In a state of last-minute panic, the son pleaded with his parents to help him. Wanting to protect him from failure, they dropped everything they were doing at the eleventh hour and ran out to three different stores to get all the ingredients they needed. They stayed up till very late making the dish and woke up the next morning exhausted. Sound familiar? While your intentions are good, what you're doing is reinforcing a few problematic behaviors:

- Lack of Consequences: Your child learns there are no real consequences for procrastination or poor planning.

- Last-Minute Requests: They believe that telling you things at the last minute is acceptable.

- Parental Rescue: They rely on you to solve their problems rather than learning to address them independently.

Shifting the Responsibility: Asking the Right Questions

Instead of jumping in to save the day, try shifting the responsibility back to your child. Ask questions that encourage them to reflect on their actions and think critically about how to avoid similar situations in the future:

You: "When was this project assigned?"

Child: "Two weeks ago."

You: "Why did you choose not to tell me before now?"

Child: "I forgot."

You: "How much notice do you think is reasonable for me to get the supplies you need for a school project?"

Follow up with more questions to help them develop a plan for the next time:

- "What can you do to remember that time window better next time?"

- "What will your plan look like when you receive the next assignment?"

- "How are you going to stick with this plan in the future?"

By asking these questions, you're helping your child take ownership of their responsibilities and develop strategies for success.

Letting Them Take the Lead: Shared Goals and Independent Solutions

Once you've agreed on a shared goal—maintaining a certain GPA, managing their gaming time, or improving their behavior—it's time to let your child take the lead. Tell them it's up to them to figure out how to achieve that goal and that you're looking forward to hearing their suggestions.

For example, if the goal is to maintain a 3.0 GPA, ask them to think about it and then outline the steps they plan to take to achieve it. Encourage them to develop a clear, realistic plan and share it with you.

The Hardest Part: Holding Your Tongue

For many parents, the most challenging part of this approach is holding back. You might have great ideas for quick solutions, but resisting the urge to share them is crucial. Patience is key here. Remember, your child is likelier to make lasting changes if they "own" the solutions.

Don't push them for an immediate update. Instead, agree on a timeline: "When do you want to talk again about the solutions you've come up with?" Give them a few days to think it over, but don't wait too long—within a week, you should have a clear strategy to try.

Continuing the Journey: Building on What You've Learned

As you wait for your child to come up with their solutions, don't abandon the valuable work you've done. The strategies you've learned—asking open-ended questions and practicing reflective listening—will continue to serve you well as you move into the next phase of helping your child manage their gaming habits and other behaviors.

Remember, the ultimate goal is to lay the foundation for setting and keeping boundaries while empowering your child to become independent, responsible, and capable of solving their own problems. It's a process that takes time, but the results are well worth the effort.

Chapter Thirteen

Common Boundary Pitfalls: How to Avoid Them with Your Child

Let's face it: parenting in today's digital world is a whole new ballgame. Our challenges—especially around setting and enforcing boundaries—are uncharted territory. No generation before us has dealt with the unique blend of social media, video games, and constant online connectivity that our kids are navigating. So, take a deep breath and cut yourself some slack. When your child's tantrums hit because of the new boundaries you're trying to set, remind yourself that you're their parent, not their best friend. In these moments, your job is to be their compass, guiding them through the storm. When in doubt, pause, breathe, and ask yourself what your child needs from you as their parent.

Stick with What Works: Consistency is Key

One mistake many parents make is abandoning what's been working. Imagine you've been implementing a strategy with your child that's brought real progress. Then, suddenly, you decide to switch gears because you feel things are going well. Big mistake. It's like a patient in therapy who, after months of successful treatment, decides to stop their medication because they feel better. More often than not, they'll find themselves right back where they started.

The same principle applies to parenting. If a particular approach has been effective, stick with it. Don't stop now just because things are improving—consistency is your best friend.

Stay Firm: Emphasize Restraint, Not Restriction

As your child grows, the way you enforce boundaries must evolve. Your focus should shift from strict restriction to teaching restraint. It's about instilling values and discipline to guide them to make the right choices. Here's a surprising insight: many young adults aged 18 to 24 often regret that their parents weren't stricter with them about gaming. They wish someone had stepped in earlier to help curb their excessive gaming habits.

Remember, setting a boundary and enforcing it are two different things that shouldn't happen simultaneously. Don't create a new rule and punish your child for breaking it immediately—it's a recipe for resentment. Instead, ensure the boundaries you set are reasonable and sustainable.

Love, Boundaries, and the Risk of Clouded Judgment

We all want our kids to be happy. It's tempting to bend the rules when they're good or particularly sweet. But here's the thing— letting love override logic can be a significant pitfall in boundary setting. The desire to reward good behavior is natural, but true love means setting your child up to thrive long-term. That might mean sticking to the rules even when it's tough.

Weekly check-ins are a great way to channel that love—use these moments to reinforce why the boundaries are there and how they benefit your child. Remember, loving your child means helping them grow into the best version of themselves, including sticking to your set boundaries.

The Fear Factor: Setting Boundaries Out of Anxiety

When fear drives your decisions, you're likely to set too tight boundaries. If you're worried that your child is heading down a dangerous path, your reaction might be to clamp down hard with strict rules. But here's the problem: your child may not see the situation as you do, leading to confusion and rebellion.

Boundaries based on fear often feel disconnected from your child's reality. They won't understand why you're so worked up, and they'll react to what they perceive as irrational behavior. To avoid this, make sure your boundaries are grounded in the reality of your child's behavior, not your worst fears.

Getting on the Same Page with Your Spouse: Presenting a United Front

Parenting is a team sport, and you and your spouse or co-parent need to be on the same page regarding boundaries. Differences in perspective are natural—after all, they might be part of what drew you together in the first place. However, a united front is crucial regarding parenting, especially in areas like gaming.

Start with open-ended questions: "What do you think about our child's gaming?" Listen carefully to their response and use reflective listening to ensure you truly understand their point of view. Then, share your concerns in a way that invites dialogue rather than debate. The goal isn't to prove who's right but to find common ground.

Dealing with Dueling Households: Navigating Inconsistent Rules

Things get even trickier when co-parenting from separate households or dealing with other caregivers like grandparents or ex-spouses. When the rules aren't consistent, kids quickly learn to play one side against another. This dynamic can lead to a situation where addiction or bad habits thrive because boundaries aren't consistently enforced.

The key here is communication. If possible, sit down with all the key players—whether it's your ex, your parents, or your child's friends' parents—and agree on a set of common rules. This might involve some tough conversations, but it's essential to create a united front. The more consistent the boundaries, the better your child's chance of success.

Grandparents: Balancing Love with Limits

Grandparents can be another tricky element in the boundary-setting equation. Many see their role as one of indulgence, showering their grandchildren with gifts and affection. But when those gifts come in the form of a new video game or console, it can undermine the boundaries you're trying to set.

It's important to remember that today's grandparents didn't grow up with the kind of technology we have now—they might not fully understand the addictive nature of modern games. Approach these conversations empathetically, explaining your concerns and the reasons behind your boundaries. If necessary, set firm limits on what gifts are acceptable or when and where the grandchild-grandparent interactions can occur.

Talking with Your Child's Friends' Parents: Building a Community of Boundaries

Your child's friends and parents can be allies or obstacles in maintaining healthy boundaries. Having an open dialogue with the parents of your child's friends can help create a supportive community where everyone is on the same page.

Consider organizing a group conversation—whether over dinner, on a conference call, or via group text—to discuss your gaming concerns. Reflective listening can be a powerful tool, allowing you to understand each parent's perspective and work together to set group rules that everyone can enforce.

Boundaries are a Form of Love

Setting boundaries is one of the most challenging yet essential parts of parenting. It's about guiding your child with love, not control, and helping them develop the discipline they need to thrive. Remember that you're not alone, while the process can be fraught with difficulties—especially in today's digital age. With consistency, communication, and a united front, you can help your child navigate these challenges and grow into a well-rounded, healthy adult.

In the end, boundaries aren't just rules—they're expressions of your love and commitment to your child's well-being. Stick with what works, stay firm yet flexible, and always keep the bigger picture in mind. You've got this.

Chapter Fourteen

Reversing the Adolescent Mental Health Crisis

As we described in Chapter 4, adolescents today are experiencing an unprecedented mental health crisis. This troubling trend coincides with a major shift in how young people engage with the world—moving away from real-life play-based childhoods to screen-based lives dominated by smartphones and social media apps.

The impact of this shift is undeniable and profound. As children and teenagers spend more time glued to their phones, they are exposed to endless streams of social media, video games, and even pornography. These activities increasingly replace healthy pursuits, such as face-to-face interactions with friends and family, exercise, sleep, and reading books. The result is a rise in anxiety, depression, loneliness, and even dangerous behaviors like self-harm.

The Challenge for Parents

Many parents feel overwhelmed and helpless in the face of this crisis. They don't want their children to spend all day staring at screens, but they are also hesitant to let their kids engage in more adventurous or independent activities in the "real world." Concerns about safety, societal pressure, and the fear of their child being socially isolated if they don't have a phone or access to social media make it difficult to set boundaries.

However, if we are to reverse the disturbing trend of rising teen anxiety and depression, parents must take action. While it won't happen overnight, there are several steps that, if collectively adopted by families, could significantly reduce mental health struggles in children within just two years.

Practical Steps to Reverse the Crisis

1. Delay Access to Smartphones

Children should not have access to smartphones until they reach high school. Smartphones are powerful tools, but they are not necessary for younger children and can prematurely introduce them to unhealthy online environments.

If a child needs a phone in middle school, it should be a flip phone or smartwatch without access to apps or the internet. No phones before middle school.

2. Delay Access to Social Media

Social media should be off-limits until children are at least sixteen years old. Research has shown that social media can contribute to negative body image, anxiety, and depression in teens. Snapchat, in particular, should be delayed until college, as it is particularly prone to creating issues of comparison and social pressure.

3. Implement Phone-Free Schools

Schools should adopt phone-free policies during the school day. Locking away phones can encourage students to engage with their peers face-to-face and focus on their education without the distraction of social media and messaging apps.

4. Encourage More Independence

Allow children more independence and opportunities for free play. Giving kids responsibilities and encouraging them to explore the world outside their screens advances confidence and resilience. It also helps them develop problem-solving and social skills.

5. Prioritize Real-World Experiences

Ensure that children have plenty of real-world experiences with friends. Instead of defaulting to screen time, encourage activities like meeting up with friends, playing sports, or engaging in creative hobbies. These experiences build meaningful relationships and offer an outlet for stress.

6. Promote Unsupervised Play

Unsupervised play is crucial for childhood development. Allowing kids the freedom to explore and play without constant adult intervention nurtures imagination, promotes decision-making, and offers opportunities for cooperation with peers.

7. Encourage Participation in Communal Activities

Drama, music groups, sports, and clubs provide structured environments where kids can engage with their peers and develop a sense of belonging. These activities are crucial for promoting teamwork and reducing feelings of isolation.

8. Set Tech Boundaries in the Home

Establish household tech boundaries. Limiting screen time for the entire family, creating tech-free zones, and setting specific times when technology is off-limits (such as during meals) can help children learn to manage their screen use.

9. Implement Phone-Free Fridays

Commit to having phone-free Fridays or designate one day each week when the family disconnects from devices. This can create opportunities for family bonding, physical activity, and stress relief.

The adolescent mental health crisis cannot be ignored, but it can be addressed. While technology and smartphones are here to stay, they should not dominate children's lives at the expense of their mental well-being. Parents, educators, and communities must actively create healthier environments for our kids—ones that prioritize real-world experiences, personal growth, and genuine connection over endless screen time.

We can turn this crisis around by delaying access to smartphones and social media, setting boundaries, and promoting more meaningful, real-life experiences. In time, these steps will help reduce anxiety and depression among adolescents, ensuring they grow up with the tools they need to thrive in a complex, digital world.

Chapter Fifteen

Recognizing When to Seek Professional Help for Your Child

A s a parent, one of the most challenging questions you may face is knowing when to seek professional help for your child. The signs of a serious issue can sometimes be subtle, and it's natural to wonder if what you see is just a phase or something more concerning. But how do you know when to call in a professional? Let's break down what "serious" means and the signs you should look for.

Signs That Things Are Serious

Certain behaviors and changes in your child are clear indicators of serious issues that warrant professional intervention. Here are some examples that most parents—and professionals—would consider serious:

1. Impaired Academic Functioning

One of the first red flags is a noticeable decline in your child's academic performance. This might show up as slipping grades or reports from teachers and school administrators about your child's sudden drop in academic engagement. If your child's schoolwork is suffering, it's a sign that something deeper might be going on.

2. Changes in Friendships or Family Relationships

Social relationships are crucial during a child's development. If your child suddenly has a falling out with a longtime friend or begins hanging out with a new, unfamiliar crowd, this could cause concern. Similarly, it's worth paying attention if family relationships have become noticeably strained or tense.

3. The Absence of Real-Life Friends

A lack of real-life social connections is another serious indicator. If your child doesn't seem to have any close friends or spends most of their time alone, it could point to underlying emotional or psychological issues that need addressing.

4. Extreme Isolation

Isolation goes beyond just spending time alone—it's about withdrawing entirely from family activities and social interactions. If your child stays in their room all day, skipping meals, or avoids interaction with others, it's a sign that something is wrong.

5. Extreme Dependence

While some dependence is normal, extreme reliance on others for basic tasks—like getting out of bed, cleaning up, or cooking—can signal deeper issues. If your child struggles to manage daily responsibilities, it may be time to seek help.

6. Tantrums and Destructive Behavior

We all know that kids can have tantrums, but when these outbursts become extreme—reaching the point of breaking things—it's a signal that your child is struggling to manage their emotions.

7. Frequent Arguments

If daily or frequent arguments occur between your child and other family members, it's a sign of deeper conflict that may need professional intervention. Constant conflict can take a toll on the entire family's well-being.

8. Rebellious Behavior

Rebellion is common when growing up, but behaviors like sneaking out at night or repeatedly breaking family rules are serious. These actions indicate that your child might be testing boundaries in dangerous ways.

9. Self-Harm

Any form of self-harm is a critical red flag. This can include drug use, excessive drinking, disordered eating, or physical self-harm like cutting. These behaviors indicate that your child is distressed and needs immediate help.

10. Physical Fights

If your child is getting into physical fights, whether at school or home, this is a serious behavioral issue. Harming others is never acceptable, and it's a clear sign that your child may be struggling with anger, frustration, or other deep-seated issues.

11. Suicidal or Homicidal Thoughts

The most serious red flag of all is if your child expresses suicidal or homicidal thoughts or behaviors. This is an emergency that requires immediate medical evaluation. Never ignore or downplay these statements—they are always serious and should be treated as such.

When to Take Action

If any behaviors on the above list are more than infrequent, it's time to take action. Trust your instincts—things are likely serious if you notice these signs. It's better to seek professional help sooner rather than later. Even if your first visit to a professional is just for an evaluation, it's a proactive step that can provide critical insights into your child's needs.

The Importance of Early Intervention

Taking action early can make all the difference. The earlier you seek help, the better equipped you'll be to support your child and address any issues before they escalate. Knowledge is power, and consulting with professionals gives you the tools and under-standing needed to guide your child through their struggles.

Remember, seeking help is not a sign of failure—it's a sign of strength and dedication to your child's well-being. Whether the issues are academic, social, emotional, or behavioral, professional guidance can provide the support and strategies your family needs to navigate these challenges effectively.

Chapter Sixteen
Resources for Finding Professional Help: A Guide for Parents

When it comes to navigating the complexities of parenting in today's digital world, seeking professional help can be a game-changer. Whether you're dealing with tech addiction or behavioral issues or need some extra support, finding the right help is crucial. But where do you start? Here's a breakdown of some top resources and tips to guide your journey.

Finding the Right Therapist: It's All About Fit

When finding a therapist, the most important factor is fit. Research shows that the success of a therapeutic relationship isn't necessarily tied to the therapist's credentials, years of experience, or cultural background. Instead, it's about how comfortable you and your child feel with the therapist.

Don't be discouraged if it takes a few tries to find the right match. It's common to meet with one to three professionals before finding someone who clicks with your family. The right therapist can make all the difference in your child's journey toward better mental health and well-being.

If you're ready to seek in-person professional support, here are some practical steps to help you get started:

1. Speak to a Medical Professional

Your first port of call can be your family doctor or pediatrician. Doctors are well-connected in the healthcare community and can often refer you to a trusted therapist or specialist. Don't hesitate to ask them for recommendations—they're there to help.

2. Talk to Your Child's School Counselor

School counselors are valuable resources for addressing tech addiction or other behavioral concerns. They work closely with children and are often familiar with local resources that can provide the support your child needs. Reach out to them and explain your concerns; they may have some excellent recommendations.

3. Leverage Your Personal Network

Sometimes, the best leads come from those closest to you. Ask your family and friends if they know of any good therapists. Personal recommendations can be incredibly valuable because they come from people you trust.

4. Use the Internet

The internet is a powerful tool for finding healthcare providers. Start by searching for "therapist" or "psychiatrist" in your area. Websites like Psychology Today offer directories of licensed professionals, complete with reviews and detailed profiles. If a particular office isn't accepting new patients, don't hesitate to ask them for other recommendations—they may know someone who is.

5. Contact Your Insurance Provider

Your insurance provider can be a great resource if you're in a country with an insurance-based medical system. They can provide a list of approved therapists in your area, ensuring you're covered and saving you from out-of-pocket expenses.

Finding the right help for your child is a journey, and taking your time is okay. Trust your instincts, and don't be afraid to shop around until you find the right fit. Whether tapping into online communities or consulting with professionals, the most important thing is that you're taking steps to support your child's well-being.

Please remember that you should try to find help, not weakness. You're doing what's best for your child, and that's something to be proud of.

Chapter Seventeen

Final Thoughts: Take Your Time and Trust the Process

Congratulations on starting a journey to connect with your child. With how different your child's life is from the one you had growing up, this journey can be challenging. You should expect bumps on the road. Don't overwhelm yourself trying all the negotiation techniques at once. Try one communication technique at a time. If your first attempt at using the communication techniques you learned in this book did not work perfectly, that is okay. Try again, and don't be afraid to mess up. When I graduated from crisis negotiation school, I wasn't an expert at my job yet. It took a lot of practice before I got on a phone with a barricaded subject. The communication techniques in this book are skills. And like all skills, they get better with use.

Be patient with your child and especially with yourself. Celebrate the small wins and build on them. Seek professional help when you feel overwhelmed. Most of all, your child is worth it.

Chapter Eighteen
Tools and Resources

About Cyber Safety Cop

Established in 2012, Cyber Safety Cop has been a leader in Safety Education and Awareness. We take pride in being pioneers in school safety education and awareness programs. Our expert team has designed courses that address the ever-evolving challenges of the digital age. We ensure that our programs are always relevant, engaging, and effective by staying ahead of the curve. Experienced Instructors: Our team is made up of seasoned professionals with diverse law enforcement and education backgrounds. Each instructor brings extensive experience working with students and families, enabling them to connect with their audiences on a personal level. We understand the unique dynamics of classrooms and workplaces, allowing us to tailor our approach to fit the specific needs of each audience.

Global Reach: Although based in Southern California, our impact knows no boundaries. Our programs are delivered internationally, reaching individuals and organizations worldwide. Whether through conferences, seminars, or online training, we are committed to spreading our knowledge far and wide.

Boundary Plan Worksheet

Download from our website at: www.cybersafetycop.com/downloads.

Join Our Membership Program

Are you a concerned parent, educator, or caregiver seeking to safeguard your children from the digital world's ever-evolving dangers? Online safety issues constantly change in today's technology-driven era, making shielding our children from potential threats challenging. Our membership program is your ultimate solution for overcoming daily challenges and effectively protecting your loved ones.

Membership includes:

- 30-minute one-on-one consultation with Clayton Cranford

- Exclusive Blog Articles

- Access to our all of our online courses

- Monthly recorded webinar training

- Monthly live Zoom trainings

- Access to our free parent support group

- Free resources like parental control guides and in-depth app reviews

- Timely and relevant advice delivered weekly to your inbox

- Access to our best eBooks

- Receive a free copy of the Parenting in the Digital World

Assemblies for Students

Cyber Safety Assembly for Students

Cyber Safety assemblies are age-appropriate 40-minute interactive presentations for students in grades K to 12th. They can be taught in small groups, a classroom, or an auditorium to hundreds of students. Our presentations address three key online safety issues all children experience: the dangers of sharing personal information with strangers, anti-bullying strategies, and how to create a positive online reputation.

Vaping, Marijuana, and Fentanyl Assembly for Students

Amid concerning trends in adolescent vaping, marijuana use, and fentanyl-related incidents, schools must prioritize the "Truth about Vaping, Marijuana, and Fentanyl" assembly for grades 6 to 12. Our impactful 45-minute presentation is a critical defense against prevailing misconceptions about the safety of these substances. By confronting realities, this session dismantles myths and highlights the risks associated with teen vaping, marijuana, and fentanyl use in the US.

Seminars for Parents

Cyber Safety Seminar For Parents

Based on Clay Cranford's acclaimed book Parenting in the Digital World, this 90-minute seminar will prepare parents to supervise their children on social media sites effectively, protect them from online threats, and restore technological balance to their homes. Law enforcement officers and educators with extensive experience working with children teach the presentation.

Vaping, Marijuana, and Fentanyl Assembly for Parents

Our concern for the safety and well-being of our children is paramount. In response to the alarming rise in teen vaping, marijuana use, and fentanyl-related deaths, we present a thought-provoking 90-minute session designed specifically for parents. This presentation will equip parents with the essential knowledge to protect their children and engage in meaningful conversations about substance use and addiction.

Online Classes

Digital Parenting 101

In today's digital world, ensuring your child's online safety is paramount. Join expert instructor Clayton Cranford in this comprehensive course designed to equip parents with the knowledge and tools to protect their children from online threats and allow for a positive digital experience.

With Clayton's extensive expertise in internet safety and child protection, you'll gain insights into crucial topics such as cyberbullying, online predators, screen time, and sensitive conversations about pornography and substance abuse.

By the end of this , you'll be equipped with the tools and knowledge needed to guide your child through the digital landscape while ensuring their safety, well-being, and positive online experiences.

Digital Citizenship for Students 1st – 3rd Grade

In today's tech-focused world, we must introduce digital citizenship education to young students using a turnkey program. This ensures online safety foundations and skill integration at home and school.

This online course includes 6 video lessons, plus accompanying worksheets and a teacher's guide.

Digital Citizenship for Students 4th – 8th Grade

Our tailored program equips young learners with essential skills to navigate the digital world responsibly.

OurPact App

OurPact is a comprehensive parental control app designed to help parents manage their children's online activities and ensure their safety. Key features include app blocking, internet filtering, text message blocking, and screen time scheduling. With the ability to manage up to 20 devices, OurPact provides customizable controls, making it an excellent choice for parents who want to protect their children from harmful content and excessive screen time.

Endnotes

[1] Cell phone ownership. (2012). Retrieved from https://www.pewresearch.org/internet/2012/03/19/cell-phone-ownership/

[2] (N.d.). Retrieved from https://www.commonsensemedia.org/sites/default/files/research/report/census_researchreport.pdf

[3] (N.d.). Retrieved from https://www.commonsensemedia.org/sites/default/files/research/report/2023-cs-smartphone-research-report_final-for-web.pdf

[4] Liu J, Chen X, Lewis G. Childhood internalizing behaviour: analysis and implications. J Psychiatr Ment Health Nurs. 2011 Dec;18(10):884-94. doi: 10.1111/j.1365-2850.2011.01743.x. Epub 2011 May 20. PMID: 22070805; PMCID: PMC5675073.

[5] Samek DR, Hicks BM. Externalizing Disorders and Environmental Risk: Mechanisms of Gene-Environment Interplay and Strategies for Intervention. Clin Pract (Lond). 2014;11(5):537-547. doi: 10.2217/CPR.14.47. PMID: 25485087; PMCID: PMC4255466.

[6] Kovess-Masfety V, Woodward MJ, Keyes K, Bitfoi A, Carta MG, Koç C, Lesinskiene S, Mihova Z, Otten R, Husky M. Gender, the gender gap, and their interaction; analysis of relationships with children's mental health problems. Soc Psychiatry Psychiatr Epidemiol. 2021 Jun;56(6):1049-1057. doi: 10.1007/s00127-020-01950-5. Epub 2020 Sep 10. Erratum in: Soc Psychiatry Psychiatr Epidemiol. 2022 Jan;57(1):219. doi: 10.1007/s00127-021-02180-z. PMID: 32914299; PMCID: PMC7943656.

[7] Substance Abuse and Mental Health Services Administration. DSM-5 Changes: Implications for Child Serious Emotional Disturbance [Internet]. Rockville (MD): Substance Abuse and Mental Health Services Administration (US); 2016 Jun. Table 16, DSM-IV to DSM-5 Social Phobia/Social Anxiety Disorder Comparison. Available from: https://www.ncbi.nlm.nih.gov/books/NBK519712/table/ch3.t12/

[8] Data shows Wisconsin students face significant mental health and emotional challenges. (2022). Retrieved from https://dpi.wi.gov/news/releases/2022/youth-risk-behavior-survey-wisconsin-mental-health Similarly, a 2023 study of American college students found that 37% experienced anxiety "always" or "most of the time," and an additional 31% felt anxious "about half the time." Only one-third of the students reported feeling anxiety less than half the time or never.Heinze, N. research from J. (2023). College Students' Anxiety, Depression Higher Than Ever, but So Are Efforts to Receive Care: News: University of Michigan School of Public Health: Mental Health:

Healthy Minds Study. Retrieved from https://sph.umich.edu/news/2023posts/college-students-anxiety-depression-higher-than-ever-but-so-are-efforts-to-receive-care.html

[9] Symptoms, signs, and side effects of anxiety. (n.d.). Retrieved from https://www.medicalnewstoday.com/articles/322510#causes

[10] How Anxiety Impacts the Way We Perceive and Think. (n.d.). Retrieved from https://www.psychologytoday.com/us/blog/anxiety-fear-and-hate/201902/how-anxiety-impacts-the-way-we-perceive-and-think#:~:text=Robust%20evidence%20shows%20that%20anxiety,stimuli%20during%20a%20cognitive%20function.

[11] Depression. (n.d.). Retrieved from https://www.nimh.nih.gov/health/topics/depression

[12] Gratz KL, Dixon-Gordon KL, Chapman AL, Tull MT. Diagnosis and Characterization of DSM-5 Nonsuicidal Self-Injury Disorder Using the Clinician-Administered Nonsuicidal Self-Injury Disorder Index. Assessment. 2015 Oct;22(5):527-39. doi: 10.1177/1073191114565878. Epub 2015 Jan 20. PMID: 25604630; PMCID: PMC5505727.

[13] Klonsky, E. D., Victor, S. E., & Saffer, B. Y. (n.d.). Nonsuicidal self-injury: what we know, and what we need to know. Retrieved from https://www.ncbi.nlm.nih.gov/pmc/articles/PMC4244874/#b5-cjp-2014-vol59-november-565-568

[14] Neuropsychiatric Disease and Treatment downloaded from https://www.dovepress.com/ by 173.76.218.81 on 10-Apr-2020

[15] CDC WISQARS - Web-based Injury Statistics Query and Reporting System. (n.d.). Retrieved from https://wisqars.cdc.gov/

[16] Curtin, S. C., National Vital Statistics Report,Vol. 69, No. 11, 2020

[17] Stone, D. M., et al. Morbidity and Mortality Weekly Report, Vol. 72, No. 6, 2023

[18] (n.d.). Retrieved from https://www.apa.org/monitor/2023/07/psychologists-preventing-teen-suicide

[19] Cranford, C. (2024). How Selfie Filters Can Harm Self Esteem And Also Attract Predators. Retrieved from https://cybersafetycop.com/how-selfie-filters-can-harm-self-esteem-and-also-attract-predators-2/

[20] Gecker, J. (2024). Young girls are using anti-aging products they see on social media. The harm is more than skin deep. Retrieved from https://www.startribune.com/young-girls-are-using-anti-aging-products-they-see-on-social-media-the-harm-is-more-than-skin-deep/601135364

[21] Ford, C. (2024). Dopamine, explained. Retrieved from https://www.vox.com/future-perfect/24159087/what-is-dopamine-hacking-fasting-does-it-work-science

[22] Avena, N. M., Rada, P., & Hoebel, B. G. (n.d.). Evidence for sugar addiction: behavioral and neurochemical effects of intermittent, excessive sugar intake. Retrieved from https://www.ncbi.nlm.nih.gov/pmc/articles/PMC2235907/

[23] (N.d.). Retrieved from https://www.axios.com/2017/12/15/sean-parker-unloads-on-facebook-god-only-knows-what-its-doing-to-our-childrens-brains-1513306792

[24] Intermechanismcontributor. (2023). Addictive game design. Retrieved from https://intermittentmechanism.blog/2023/05/13/addictive-game-design/

[25] Volkow, N. D., Wang, G.-J., Fowler, J. S., Tomasi, D., Telang, F., & Baler, R. (n.d.). Addiction: decreased reward sensitivity and increased expectation sensitivity conspire to overwhelm the brain's control circuit. Retrieved from https://www.ncbi.nlm.nih.gov/pmc/articles/PMC2948245/

[26] Person. (2024). Video Games and Mental Health Explained. Retrieved from https://www.healthygamer.gg/blog/video-games-and-mental-health-explained#:~:text=The%20amygdala%20is%20the%20part,neg-ative%20emotions%20and%20suppress%20them.

[27] Person. (2024). Video Games and Mental Health Explained. Retrieved from https://www.healthygamer.gg/blog/video-games-and-mental-health-explained#:~:text=The%20amygdala%20is%20the%20part,neg-ative%20emotions%20and%20suppress%20them

About the Author

Clayton Cranford, founder of Cyber Safety Cop and Total Safety Solutions LLC, has dedicated his career to protecting young people and promoting safety in both the real world and the digital landscape. With over 20 years of distinguished service in law enforcement, Clayton has held pivotal roles such as School Resource Officer, Juvenile Investigator, Crisis Negotiator, and Behavioral Threat Assessor. His extensive experience in these fields has made him one of the nation's leading experts in social media safety, child protection, and behavioral threat assessments.

Clayton's commitment to keeping children safe online led him to write the authoritative guide for parents, Parenting in the Digital World. This essential book empowers parents with the knowledge and tools they need to safeguard their children from the ever-evolving dangers of the internet. As a respected educator and thought leader, Clayton continues to influence the national conversation on digital safety, helping parents and educators navigate the complexities of raising children in the digital world.

Clayton resides in Orange County, California with his wife Gretchen and his two boys, Clay and Zachary.

Made in the USA
Middletown, DE
03 February 2025

70069699R00086